Crash Course in Young Adult Services

Recent Titles in
Libraries Unlimited Crash Course Series

Crash Course in Dealing with Difficult Library Customers
Shelley E. Mosley, Dennis C. Tucker, and Sandra Van Winkle

Crash Course in Children's Services, Second Edition
Penny Peck

Crash Course in Collection Development, Second Edition
Wayne Disher

Crash Course in Marketing for Libraries, Second Edition
Susan W. Alman and Sara Gillespie Swanson

Crash Course in Readers' Advisory
Cynthia Orr

Crash Course in Storytime Fundamentals, Second Edition
Penny Peck

Crash Course in Basic Cataloging with RDA
Heather Lea Moulaison and Raegan Wiechert

Crash Course in Weeding Library Collections
Francisca Goldsmith

Crash Course in Technology Planning
Christopher D. Brown

Crash Course in Library Budgeting and Finance
Glen E. Holt and Leslie E. Holt

Crash Course in eBooks
Michele McGraw and Gail Mueller Schultz

Crash Course in Contemporary Reference
Francisca Goldsmith

Crash Course in Young Adult Services

Sarah Flowers

Crash Course

LIBRARIES
UNLIMITED™
An Imprint of ABC-CLIO, LLC
Santa Barbara, California • Denver, Colorado

Library of Congress Cataloging-in-Publication Data

Names: Flowers, Sarah, 1952– author.
Title: Crash course in young adult services / Sarah Flowers.
Description: Santa Barbara : Libraries Unlimited, [2017] | Series: Crash course | Includes
   bibliographical references and index.
Identifiers: LCCN 2017014160 (print) | LCCN 2017038317 (ebook) |
   ISBN 9781440851711 (ebook) | ISBN 9781440851704 (alk. paper)
Subjects: LCSH: Young adults' libraries—United States. | Libraries and
   teenagers—United States.
Classification: LCC Z718 (ebook) | LCC Z718 .F57 2017 (print) | DDC 027.62/6—dc23
LC record available at https://lccn.loc.gov/2017014160

ISBN: 978-1-4408-5170-4
EISBN: 978-1-4408-5171-1

21 20 19 18 17   1 2 3 4 5

This book is also available as an eBook.

Libraries Unlimited
An Imprint of ABC-CLIO, LLC

ABC-CLIO, LLC
130 Cremona Drive, P.O. Box 1911
Santa Barbara, California 93116-1911
www.abc-clio.com

This book is printed on acid-free paper ∞

Manufactured in the United States of America

CONTENTS

Introduction. vii

Chapter 1—The Teenage Years 1

Chapter 2—Positive Interactions with Teens 11

Chapter 3—Teen Collections 21

Chapter 4—Programming for Teens 35

Chapter 5—Teens and Their Information Needs 49

Chapter 6—Teen Spaces 59

Chapter 7—Speaking Up for Teens 65

Chapter 8—Teen Volunteers and Workers 75

Chapter 9—Keeping Up: Professional Resources and Development 87

Appendix A: Creating a Crash Course Workshop 97
Appendix B: Programs 103
Appendix C: Displays and Booklists 111
Further Reading 129
Index 131

INTRODUCTION

Working with teens in the library can be challenging, fun, exhilarating, frustrating, inspirational, and exhausting—sometimes all at once! In this book, I will use the terms "teens" and "young adults" interchangeably, referring to young people in adolescence—basically those from 12 to 18 years old, or from seventh grade to senior year in high school. These young people are going through massive changes in their brains and in their bodies. They are no longer children, but they aren't quite adults yet either.

The teenage years have long been recognized as difficult ones, both for teens and for the adults who deal with them. In *The Winter's Tale*, one of Shakespeare's characters says:

> I would there were no age between ten and three-and-twenty, or that youth would sleep out the rest; for there is nothing in the between but getting wenches with child, wronging the ancientry, stealing, fighting—Hark you now! Would any but these boiled brains of nineteen and two-and-twenty hunt in this weather? (Act III, Scene 3)

But they are also years of astonishing growth and development, when young people find their life's passion and begin to be recognizably the people they will become as adults. Just to give you a visual image of the changes that go on in the teen years, take a minute and think about the Harry Potter books and movies. In the first book (and movie), Harry, Ron, and Hermione were 11-year-olds, and the actors who played them in the movies were also 11 and 12 years old. By the final book in the series, they were 17, and nearly adult. In the movies, the actors were 17 and 18 years old during the fifth movie (*Harry Potter and the Half-Blood Prince*).

My own experience of working with teens has taken place in public libraries in California, as well as in my own home, where I raised three sons. I have been an active member of the Young Adult Library Services Association (YALSA) for over 20 years, including a term as YALSA president. In addition, I have been teaching online and in-person courses on working with teens in libraries for the past seven years. In all of those capacities, I have picked up information about teens that I will share with you in this book.

This book is aimed primarily at those of you who work in small or medium-sized libraries, where you are unlikely to have a dedicated teen services specialist who has training in working with teens.

In Chapter 1, we'll start by looking at the teen brain and exploring what exactly is going on during those formative years. In addition, we'll take a look at how life is different for members of the post-millennial generation than it was for their predecessors.

Chapter 2 focuses on those tough behavioral issues, and especially on how to have positive interactions with teens in the library. We'll look at how to differentiate between truly dangerous behaviors and those that are unwelcome, but merely distracting, and we'll see how teen participation in programs and services can help you help them.

Chapter 3 is about teen collections: how to find and select materials for teens, how to do readers' advisory with teens, and how to booktalk with teens. In addition, we'll look at the concept of transliteracy—the ability to read, write, and interact across a wide range of media.

In Chapter 4, I give you some tips on doing programming with and for teens, including planning, organizing, publicizing, and evaluating programs.

Chapter 5 focuses on teens and their informational needs: homework help, information literacy, using the library catalog and other resources, and dealing effectively with school assignments.

Chapter 6 looks at teen spaces and discusses how to create a teen-friendly library even when your building restricts your ability to have a dedicated teen area. We'll also look at policies and how they affect your interactions with teens in the library.

In Chapter 7, we'll look at how to advocate for teens, and how to provide them equal access to materials and services in your library. This includes a discussion about handling challenges to materials, how to manage computer use and how to speak up for teens in your library and your community.

Chapter 8 looks at the challenges and the advantages of using teens as both volunteers and workers in the library.

Chapter 9 focuses on professional development and how to keep up with teen services through reading, workshops, conferences, and associations.

YALSA, a division of the American Library Association (ALA) lists nine core professional values for the teen services profession.[1] These core values are accountability, collaboration, compassion, excellence, inclusion, innovation, integrity, professional duty, and social responsibility. In this book, we'll be talking about the ways all of these core values come into play in day-to-day interactions with teens in the library.

If you are reading this book, you have already exhibited some of these values, or at least the desire to attain them. So, let's dive in and talk about teens and libraries and how they are good for each other!

NOTE

1. See   http://www.ala.org/yalsa/core-professional-values-teen-services-profession   for the full list of core values and descriptions of how a person practicing each value will act in a library setting.

CHAPTER 1

The Teenage Years

Teens are developmentally different from both children and adults. This may sound obvious, but it is a fact that is easy to forget when the teen is standing in front of us. Sometimes we remember that same teen girl when she was a child, coming to the library for story time, and so we treat her as if she were still a child. Or perhaps, seeing that the teen boy in front of us is at full adult height, with a hint of a moustache, we assume that he is fully adult. Neither is true, and in this chapter we'll look at why that is the case, and how their developmental stage affects how they behave and respond, as well as the kinds of materials and services we provide in the library.

THE TEEN BRAIN

The brain is about 80 percent developed in adolescents. Because teenagers are often adult-sized, for many years it was thought that since their brain was large, it was also fully formed. And although, in terms of sheer capacity to learn, a teen's brain is at its peak, there are vast differences in the ways teens carry out intellectual tasks. They rely on different parts of their brain than adults do, causing, for example, decisions to be made on the basis of emotional reactions rather than calculation and reason. We know now that some parts of the brain are not fully developed until the mid-twenties.

1

Anatomy

First, a little anatomy. The brain has three main parts, each of which has subsections.

- The "hindbrain" contains the brainstem and the cerebellum, and it is responsible for the basic functions of life: breathing, heart rate, blood pressure, and so on.
- The "midbrain" contains the amygdala (which is involved in memory, emotion, and fear) and the hippocampus (which helps convert short-term memory to more long-term memory). Together the amygdala and the hippocampus form the limbic system. The midbrain also contains the hypothalamus (involved in things like hunger, thirst, and circadian rhythms) and the thalamus (containing sensory and motor functions).
- The "forebrain" is the cerebrum or cortex and is associated with higher brain functions like thought and decision. This cerebral cortex is divided into four lobes: the frontal (at the top front, behind the forehead), the parietal (at the top back), the temporal (on the sides), and the occipital (at the back of the skull). Each lobe has its own particular function. The frontal lobe contains the centers for judgment, impulse control, concentration, and planning. The parietal lobe controls movement and sensation. The temporal lobes control language, as well as emotions and sexuality, and the occipital lobe contains the visual cortex.

The Cortex

The cortex is the part of the brain that is just under the scalp and skull. The cortex is the part of the brain that we use to think, remember, plan, and make decisions. Reasoning, reflecting, remembering past events, and assessing situations are all functions of the cortex, which is sometimes called the "executive region" of the brain. In particular, the executive function occurs in the prefrontal cortex, the area just behind the forehead. As Dr. Daniel Siegel (2013, 89) says, "this prefrontal region links input from the body itself and from other people. Energy and information from the cortex, limbic area, brainstem, body, and social world are coordinated and balanced by the prefrontal region."

Siegel goes on to point out that the "overall movement of the brain's development is to become more *integrated*. What that means is that areas will become more specialized and then interconnected to one another in more effective ways." And all of this is happening during adolescence. As young teens try different experiences, discuss them with friends and family, and spend time thinking about what has happened and what they want to happen, the brain changes. The areas that are stimulated by the things we do and think about are the areas that grow and integrate with the rest of the brain. The areas that are not stimulated eventually get pruned away, which we'll discuss later.

Abstract Thought

When teens hit puberty, this development of the cortex means that they begin to develop the capability of abstract thought, moving from the purely concrete thought of younger children. As their frontal lobes grow, they are able to begin to think about thinking. This is why it is possible to teach algebra starting in the junior high school years, and why this is the age at which young people can begin to look more deeply into literature and its themes, motifs, and nuances. They begin to be able to generate big ideas—not silly ideas, like younger children, but really reasonable big ideas. The ability to understand nuance means that this is an age at which they can get truly funny. A six-year-old will tell you the same knock-knock joke over and over and think it hilarious. A 13- or 14-year-old, on the other hand, can appreciate irony and come up with a genuinely funny joke or story that relies on a deeper understanding of the world.

This same ability to have complex thoughts can lead adolescents to whole new ways of approaching the world, including the adults they deal with on a regular basis. In Chapter 2, we'll talk more about how these brain changes affect our interactions with teens.

Hormones

These areas of the brain mature at different times and can vary in size relative to one another. In general, however, they mature from back to front, which means that coordination, vision, movement, language, and emotion all mature ahead of judgment and impulse control. In addition, the sex hormones—testosterone, estrogen, and progesterone—are present in higher concentrations during adolescence, and they are linked to the parts of the brain that affect mood and emotions. As Dr. Frances Jensen (2015, 21) says:

> Sex hormones are particularly active in the limbic system, which is the emotional center of the brain. This explains in part why adolescents not only are emotionally volatile but may even seek out emotionally charged experiences—everything from a book that makes her sob to a roller coaster that makes him scream.

Ask any librarian who has worked with teenage girls, and he or she will confirm that "books that make me cry" is a common request!

Pruning

Another thing that is happening in the brain during adolescence is that the brain actually *reduces* its number of neurons (the brain's basic cells) and the connections between them (the synapses). This is called "pruning" and it happens as a result of both genetics and experience. As Dr. Daniel Siegel (2013, 82) puts it, "Attention streams energy and information through specific circuits and activates them. The more you use a circuit, the stronger it gets. The less you use a circuit, the more likely it may get pruned away during adolescence." This is why most top-level athletes, artists, musicians, for example, have begun to learn their skill before adolescence begins. It is also why teenagers are best served by being exposed to a variety of ideas and activities while their brains are still developing.

Teens really do want to learn, even if it doesn't always seem that way. But they mainly want to learn about the things that *they* want to learn about, not what adults want them to learn. Fortunately, that is a place where libraries, and especially public libraries, can help. "Libraries bridge the intersection between formal and informal learning," said one participant in Young Adult Library Services Association's (YALSA's) year-long national forum on teen and libraries (YALSA 2014, 12). By offering teens a place to expand their knowledge on whatever topics they are interested in, libraries can become a place of importance for teens, while also helping them develop those synapses in their brains.

CONNECTED LEARNING

Connected learning is a relatively new concept in working with teens, and it fits right into this moment of teen brain development. What's more, it is a model that is ideally suited for libraries and library staff. According to a report by the Connected Learning Research Network, "Connected learning is realized when a young person is able to pursue a personal interest or passion with the support of friends and caring adults, and is in turn able to link this learning and interest to academic achievement, career success or civic engagement" (Ito et al. 2013, 4). We see this happening when teens find a personal passion, which can be anything—a sport, a book, an art, a craft, or a field of science—and find ways to explore it more deeply and become involved in it. In an article in the American Library Association (ALA) YALSA's *Journal of Research on Libraries and Young Adults*, Crystle Martin gives several examples of teens who turned their passions into something that helped them in school, made friends, and even made money. A girl who was a professional wrestling fan turned her writing for the fantasy wrestling federation into a position on her school newspaper through the help of a sympathetic teacher and ultimately into a college major. A boy who loved *StarCraft II* (a science-fiction, real-time strategy game) but whose school commitments didn't allow him the time to practice and thus achieve a high rank, instead started a competitive high school *StarCraft* league and devoted himself to coaching others. In the process, he learned a lot about organization management. And a young woman who was a member of *Hogwarts at Ravelry*, a forum for people who like to knit and crochet Harry Potter-themed items, turned her passion into a job writing and selling crochet patterns (Martin 2015).

When libraries can take that teen passion to learn and help teens figure out way to connect their learning with their lives, everyone benefits: teens, libraries, and whole communities.

SLEEP DEPRIVATION

Human sleep patterns are controlled by hormones and various signals from the brain, and those patterns change throughout childhood and adolescence. Most babies and children tend to go to bed early and get up early, where teens are inclined to stay up late and sleep later in the day. Teens are often forced to wake early because of school and even before-school commitments, but getting up early does not usually result in going earlier to bed, which means that many teenagers are chronically sleep-deprived.

According to the National Sleep Foundation (NSF), "Teens need about 8 to 10 hours of sleep each night to function best. Most teens do not get enough sleep—one study found that only 15% reported sleeping 8 1/2 hours on school nights" (NSF 2016b). Sleep allows time for the body and brain to process the day's activities. Brain growth, immune system function, the ability to remember what you learned that day, the ability to focus, solve problems, and handle the emotions—all of these require adequate sleep.

Melatonin is a natural hormone that is made by the body's pineal gland, which is in the middle of the brain. The pineal gland produces melatonin, which is released into the bloodstream, causing the body to feel less alert and drowsier. Melatonin levels are high during the nighttime hours and barely detectable during the day. But whereas in adults, melatonin levels start to rise around 9 p.m., in teens, it often does not kick in until closer to 11 p.m. Not only that, but there are many factors, mostly related to light, that can inhibit melatonin production. Using electronic devices, for example, can inhibit melatonin production. According to the NSF, "The circadian rhythm seems to be especially sensitive to light with short wavelengths—in particular, blue light in the 460-nanometer range of the electromagnetic spectrum. This light, which is given off by electronics like computers and cell phones . . . has been shown to delay the release of melatonin" (NSF 2016a).

The effects of sleep deprivation are familiar to all of us: irritability, stress, low energy, short temper, and short memory. In some high schools in Minnesota, school start times were moved from 7:30 a.m. to 8:40 a.m. "Compared with students in schools that maintained the earlier start time for the school day, the students in the districts whose schools started later reported they got more sleep, earned better grades, and experienced fewer episodes of depression" (NSF 2016c).

So it's worthwhile to keep in mind that many teens may be suffering from these feelings most of the time. Added to the other changes going on in their brains and bodies, it's no wonder they are often moody and temperamental.

POST-MILLENNIALS

Today's teens fall at the tail end of the group known as millennials (those born after 1981). This is a large and diverse group and among the most ethnically and racially diverse in U.S. history. Of course, it varies widely according to region, but teens in the United States are more likely to be Asian, Hispanic, or the ever-growing "two or more races" than they are to be white.

Millennials are, as the Pew Research Center says, "the first generation in human history who regard behaviors like tweeting and texting, along with websites like Facebook, YouTube, Google and Wikipedia, not as astonishing innovations of the digital era, but as everyday parts of their social lives and their search for understanding" (Keeter and Taylor 2009). They are actually more inclined to trust in institutions than are either baby boomers or Gen Xers (those who are now 30–45 years old).

In January 2013, Lee Rainie of the Pew Internet Project made a presentation on *Teens and Libraries* for the National Forum on Teens and Libraries Summit, sponsored by YALSA. Rainie (2013) started by pointing out seven key takeaways from his research:

- Teens live in a different information ecosystem.
- Teens live in a different learning ecosystem.
- Teens' reading levels match or exceed adult reading levels.
- Teens use libraries and librarians more than others but don't necessarily love libraries as much.
- Teens have different priorities in library service.
- Teens will behave differently in the world to come.
- The public and teachers recognize this and want libraries to adjust to it.

One of the important things to remember about today's teens is that they are not having the same experience of being a teen as you had. Just in the last 10 years, things have changed in important ways. Technology has had a major impact in the lives of teens at home and at school. Teachers keep online gradebooks, and teens—and their parents—can log in at any time to see how they are doing. It is expected that students will complete assignments using word processing, spreadsheet, and presentation software. They have never known life without computers. Many are highly socially connected, using handheld devices (smartphones, tablets, e-readers, etc.). A snapshot done by Nielsen in October 2013 showed that 70 percent of American teens (ages 13–17) owned a smartphone, and the numbers are likely even higher today (The Nielsen Company 2013).

Rainie (2013) noted that in an online survey of teachers, 77 percent said that Internet and digital search tools have had a "mostly positive" impact on their students' research work, while at the same time, 87 percent agree that these technologies are creating an "easily distracted generation with short attention spans." Nevertheless, students are expected to use those digital search tools in completing assignments. In the library, you may have noticed that teens, unlike older populations, may prefer to work in group study rooms rather than at isolated study carrels and that they have a different approach to using tools like the library catalog.

In a nationwide survey of 10- to 14-year-olds done for YALSA and the Association for Library Service to Children (ALSC) in the summer of 2012, 55 percent of the respondents said they preferred reading hard-copy books, while 45 percent preferred eBooks (Poris 2012). The reason they like eBooks? Because of the flexibility: they can easily switch books or switch between reading and doing other activities, such as looking up information, playing games, or texting. In late 2014, teens in a Nielsen survey expressed a preference for print books, mainly because they like to borrow and share books, which is difficult to do in the e-format (The Nielsen Company 2014).

DIVERSITY

In 2011, the Annie E. Casey Foundation (www.aecf.org) published an analysis of data from the 2010 U.S. census. The analysis revealed that

- All of the growth in the child population since 2000 has been among groups other than non-Hispanic whites.
- Children of mixed race grew at a faster rate than any other group over the past decade, increasing by 46 percent.
- The number of Hispanic children grew by 39 percent and the number of Asian and Pacific Islander children grew by 31 percent.
- Minority children (i.e., any group other than non-Hispanic white) accounted for 46 percent of the population under 18 in 2010, compared with 39 percent in 2000 and 31 percent in 1990.
- In 10 states and Washington, D.C., non-Hispanic white children are now less than half of all children. The 10 states are Hawaii, New Mexico, California, Texas, Nevada, Arizona, Florida, Maryland, Georgia, and Mississippi. In eight states, on the other hand, non-Hispanic white children make up over 80 percent of the child population. The eight states are Vermont, West Virginia, Maine, New Hampshire, North Dakota, Iowa, Kentucky, and Montana.
- Nearly three-quarters of the child population in the 100 largest cities belong to a racial or Hispanic minority group.

Beyond racial and cultural diversity, there are other shifts in the child and teen population in recent years. For example, as YALSA's *The Future of Library Services for and with Teens* (2014, 2) points out:

- Twenty-two percent of U.S. children live in families with incomes below the federal poverty level.
- The number of unemployed youth ages 16–24 is currently 22.7 percent, an all-time high.
- Approximately 3 million teens quit school each year in the United States.
- More than 1.3 million children and teens experience homelessness each year.
- Approximately 5 percent of children ages 5–20 have a disability.

What do these numbers mean for you? First of all, bear in mind that these are all statistics and generalizations—and not descriptions of your unique community or of the one teen who is standing in front of you. That particular teen might be 13 or 17; boy or girl; straight or gay; wealthy or homeless; Evangelical or Catholic or Jewish or Hindu or atheist. He or she may be an avid reader, or may struggle with reading, or may be able to read but just prefer not to (or at least not to read books). Teens' tastes in music vary as widely as those of adults, and they can be very knowledgeable about the kind of music they do like, whether it's classical, hip-hop, classic rock, country, reggae, or some genre you've never heard of.

It will be of some help to you if you have an idea of the demographics of your community, but it's never a good idea to assume that the teen in front of you fits into any sort of niche. No one likes to be labeled, and teens are no exception. Knowing something about the ethnic, cultural, and religious groups in your community may help you understand the needs and attitudes of your library's users, especially if they differ from your own, but any individual library user may not fit into any category you are prepared for.

Teens interact with the library in many different ways. There are teens who simply want a comfortable chair in which to read, all the while keeping their eye on what is going on around them. There are teens who primarily want to hang out with friends. There are the ones who want to use the computers, game consoles, or board games. There are teens who need service hours for school and want to volunteer. And, of course, there are teens who need to use the library to find information.

Some libraries serve teens with special needs or teens in nontraditional settings, such as detention centers, group homes, alternative schools, or homeless shelters. Again, the first steps are to regard teens as individuals, to find out as much as you can about what their information needs are and to discern how the library might be able to help them.

In the case of teens with physical disabilities, the teens themselves are often extremely well informed about their disabilities, and they can tell you specifically what kind of help they do or do not need. In the case of nontraditional settings, there will usually be other youth-serving professionals involved who will be able to give you some background information and help you prepare to work with them effectively. As with any teen—or indeed any library user—the key to a good interaction is respect.

DEVELOPMENTAL ASSETS

Beginning in 1989, the Search Institute (www.search-institute.org) conducted surveys of sixth through twelfth graders in public and private schools all over the United States. In 1990, the institute first published a list of 40 "developmental assets" for adolescents, defined as "a set of skills, experiences, relationships, and behaviors that enable young people to develop into successful and contributing adults" (The Search Institute 2016a). Their studies have shown that the more assets young people have, the more likely they are to thrive and the less likely they are to engage in high-risk behaviors.

The assets are divided into "external" and "internal" assets. The external assets include support (from family, neighborhood, school, and other caring adults), empowerment, boundaries and expectations (from parents, school, neighborhood, peers, and other adults), and constructive use of time (in creative activities, clubs or sports, religious activities, and at home). The internal assets fall into the areas of commitment to learning (including engagement in school and reading for pleasure), positive values (including integrity, honesty, responsibility, and social justice), social competencies (including planning and decision-making, conflict resolution, and familiarity and ease with other cultures), and positive identity (including self-esteem and sense of purpose) (The Search Institute 2016b).

In the nearly 30 years since the assets were first defined, youth-serving professionals of all types, including library workers, have used them as a basis for planning and defending programs for teens. The library can provide some of the external assets in the areas of support, empowerment, boundaries and expectations, and constructive use of time. These, in turn, allow teens to develop the internal assets in the areas of commitment to learning, positive values, social competencies, and positive identity. Being familiar with the developmental assets can give you a common language with other people in your community who are dedicated to serving youth, and they can help you make the case for why libraries do teen services at all!

CONCLUSION

Because teens are at a unique developmental stage, they deserve unique library services. It can be tempting to lump teen services in with children's services or adult services, but it is clear from the research that teens are neither children nor adults. Library services that take into account the needs of teens are library services that will be the most effective for the community as a whole. When we recognize that teens, as Daniel Siegel (2013, 7) says, "seek rewards in trying new things, connect with their peers in different ways, feel more intense emotions, and push back on the existing ways of doing things to create new ways of being in the world," then it can color the ways in which we design collections, spaces, programs, and services for teens in the library. Even knowing just a bit about teen development can help library workers provide a supportive, positive library experience for teens, and that in turn can be a positive influence on the community as a whole.

REFERENCES

AECF (The Annie E. Casey Foundation). November 2011. "The Changing Child Population of the United States." Available at: http://www.aecf.org/m/resourcedoc/AECF-ChangingChildPopulation-2011-Full.pdf.

Ito, Mizuko, et al. 2013. *Connected Learning: An Agenda for Research and Design*. Irvine, CA: Digital Media and Learning Research Hub. Available at: http://dmlhub.net/wp-content/uploads/files/Connected_Learning_report.pdf.

Jensen, Frances E., and Amy Ellis Nutt. 2015. *The Teenage Brain: A Neuroscientist's Guide to Raising Adolescents and Young Adults*. New York: Harper.

Keeter, Scott, and Paul Taylor. December 10, 2009. "The Millennials: A Portrait of Generation Next." Available at: http://www.pewresearch.org/2009/12/10/the-millennials/.

Martin, Crystle. March 2015. "Connected Learning, Librarians, and Connecting Youth Interests." *The Journal of Research on Libraries and Young Adults*. Available at: http://www.yalsa.ala.org/jrlya/2015/03/connected-learning-librarians-and-connecting-youth-interest/.

National Sleep Foundation. 2016a. "How Electronics Affect Sleep." Available at: https://sleepfoundation.org/bedroom/see.php.

National Sleep Foundation. 2016b. "Teens and Sleep." Available at: https://sleepfoundation.org/sleep-topics/teens-and-sleep.

National Sleep Foundation. 2016c. "Teens, School, and Sleep: A Complex Relationship." Available at: https://sleepfoundation.org/sleep-news/teens-school-and-sleep-complex-relationship.

The Nielsen Company. October 29, 2013. "Ring the Bells: More Smartphones in Students' Hands Ahead of Back-to-School Season." Available at: http://www.nielsen.com/us/en/insights/news/2013/ring-the-bells-more-smartphones-in-students-hands-ahead-of-back.html.

The Nielsen Company. December 9, 2014. "Don't Judge a Book by Its Cover: Tech-Savvy Teens Remain Fans of Print Books." Available at: http://www.nielsen.com/us/en/insights/news/2014/dont-judge-a-book-by-its-cover-tech-savvy-teens-remain-fans-of-print-books.html.

Poris, Michele. July 11, 2012. "The Lives of Tweens and Young Teens." Available at: http://ala12.scheduler.ala.org/files/ala12/AN12%20Smarty%20Pants%20Poris%20Presentation.pdf.

Rainie, Lee. January 23, 2013. "Teens and Libraries." Available at: http://www.pewinternet.org/2013/01/23/teens-and-libraries/.

The Search Institute. 2016a. "40 Developmental Assets for Adolescents." Available at: http://www.search-institute.org/content/40-developmental-assets-adolescents-ages-12-18.

The Search Institute. 2016b. "Developmental Assets." Available at: http://www.search-institute.org/research/developmental-assets.

Siegel, Daniel. 2013. *Brainstorm: The Power and Purpose of the Teenage Brain*. New York: JeremyTarcher/Penguin.

YALSA. 2014. "The Future of Library Services for and with Teens: A Call to Action." Available at: http://www.ala.org/yaforum/sites/ala.org.yaforum/files/content/YALSA_nationalforum_Final_web_0.pdf.

CHAPTER 2

Positive Interactions with Teens

Teens are quick to perceive injustice, disrespect, and incompetence, so it's best not to give them an opportunity to see those things. You don't need to learn new skills to work well with teens in the library so much as you need to be mindful of employing skills you are likely to have already. These include:

- Being friendly and helpful
- Being honest
- Being fair
- Being flexible
- Being clear with all of your messages
- Keeping your sense of humor
- Being open-minded and empathetic
- Knowing your library and its collections and knowing how to use the library's technology
- Treating everyone, including teens, with respect
- Learning the names of the regular library users

TEEN DEVELOPMENT AFFECTS BEHAVIOR

In Chapter 1, we learned about some of the ways that teen brains are changing and growing. These changes can directly affect the way teens behave. Knowing the reasons behind the behavior doesn't necessarily make it less irritating, but it may make you better able to take a step back and not react immediately.

For example, as the cerebral cortex grows, teens are developing critical thinking skills and the ability to think abstractly. This can be exciting when they are able to read a novel critically but less fun when that criticism is turned onto you or other adults. It may seem as if a teen is contradicting you, not because he or she particularly cares, but because he or she can. And that may be the case. By arguing with you, pointing out discrepancies in what you say, even going off on side issues, the teen is stretching his or her mind and learning how to reason. It may be hard being the one who is taking the brunt of it, but you can reassure yourself that it is helping the teen's brain and will be useful in his later life!

One of the "jobs" of the adolescent is to establish a sense of identity. Using their newly improved cognitive skills, they are able to sort through various possible futures and to analyze what their specific skills, abilities, values, attributes, beliefs, and interests are. As the American Psychological Association (APA) puts it, "The process by which an adolescent begins to achieve a realistic sense of identity also involves experimenting with different ways of appearing, sounding, and behaving. Each adolescent approaches these tasks in his or her own unique way" (APA 2002, 15).

This experimentation may mean that one teen is totally focused on a particular interest, like music, or dance, or robotics, while another may be more involved in creating a certain "look" by the way he or she dresses, wears his or her hair, and so on. One important thing to realize about this kind of experimentation is that it means that the teen feels secure enough to explore the unknown and try something different. The APA (2002, 15) points out:

> Although it may seem a simple strategy, professionals can help adolescents begin to define their identity through the simple process of taking time to ask questions and listen without judgment to the answers. It is amazing how many youth are hungry to discuss these issues with a trusted adult, and how few are offered the opportunity. Discussing these issues can also help adolescents to develop their new abstract reasoning skills and moral reasoning abilities.

This role of trusted adult is one that librarians are perfectly placed for. Listening non-judgmentally to teens lets them know that they have valuable opinions and are worth listening to. Spending time talking to the teens in our libraries is one way to help them grow, but it is also a way to help forestall future problems. If the teens regard you as a trusted adult, they will be less likely to cause trouble and more likely to exert peer pressure on other teens to keep them in line as well.

TALKING TO TEENS

By engaging teens in the library in conversation, you will learn more about them, and they will have a better feeling about the library. This does not mean, of course, inserting yourself into their conversations with one another or involving yourself in a bossy or inquisitive way. But there are many opportunities to have discussions with teens, such as when you are doing reference or readers' advisory. Teens are often happy to share their expertise, so if one is asking for help in finding materials on a topic of interest, it is an opportunity for you to probe a little, find out what they know, and what they want to know.

Ask open-ended questions, rather than yes/no questions; this will open the chance for them to talk more, and it will also give them a chance to use those cognitive skills to think through various options and ideas.

Try to avoid asking "why" questions, which can sound accusatory. So when doing a reference interview, rather than asking, "Why do you need that?" say instead, "Can you tell me more about what it is you need? Is this for a report, or are you just interested?" And when dealing with a behavior issue, the same thing goes. Instead of saying, "Why did you do that?" put it in terms of what you observed: "You really seemed angry with your friends when you did that. Can you tell me a little more about what was going on just then?"

When possible, try to mirror the teen's emotional level—be enthusiastic when he or she is enthusiastic, casual when the teen is casual, and so on. This will help the teen feel that he or she is being understood. Of course, this does not hold true if the teen is acting hostile or aggressive; in that case, you want to dial it way back down and be as calm as possible. (But do try to avoid saying "calm down": in the history of conflict, saying "calm down" never calmed anyone down!)

In a conflict situation, give teens an opportunity to think through the options and offer their own solutions. You can model this by defining the problem, anticipating positive and negative outcomes, and reaching a conclusion.

For example, suppose a group of teens are using the library computers and it's just getting louder and louder, until finally you witness one teen shoving another and calling him or her a foul name. You can approach the teen who did the shoving, pull that teen aside from the others, and say, "I see that there are a lot of kids here trying to use the computers at the same time. I know it can be frustrating, especially if you are trying to finish a project and someone else keeps interrupting you and trying to take over the keyboard. But I'm sure you realize that shoving and name-calling are not good options. For one thing, they don't solve the problem, and for another, you know that you are likely to get kicked out of the library for the day. But let's think about your options, now that you have already caused an uproar. One, you can go back, apologize, and finish your project; the staff will help enforce the computer rules, and get your friend signed up for his own computer time. Or two, you can continue to be angry, in which case I'm going to have to ask you to leave the library for at least an hour. You can go outside, run off some energy, get a snack, or whatever, but just don't come back until you are ready to abide by the rules."

FACIAL EXPRESSIONS

One interesting but little-known aspect of adolescent development is that while the brain is growing and changing, teens "find it hard to recognize others' emotions. If you show teenagers pictures of faces, they will be some 20% less accurate in gauging the emotions depicted, not recovering this ability until they are 18 or so" (Parry 2005). Have you ever looked at a teen with what you thought was a completely neutral expression, only to have her shout at you, "Why are you looking at me like that?! Why are you being mean to me?" This is perfectly normal, although admittedly a bit aggravating.

According to Dr. Daniel Siegel (2013, 107):

When teens are shown a neutral face in a photograph, a major area of the limbic region, the amygdala, becomes activated, while in adults the same photograph merely activates the reasoning prefrontal cortex. The result for teens can be an inner sense of conviction that even another person's neutral response is filled with hostility and he cannot be trusted. A blank expression or a bump in the hallway can be interpreted as intentional, and a teen may respond with an irritated remark even if the look or bump was completely innocent.

DEALING WITH TEEN BEHAVIOR

Whenever possible, learn the names of the teens in your library—especially the troublemakers! They may have the unrealistic sense that because they are in a public place, they can get away with things that they wouldn't be able to get away with in their home or at school. Calling them by name personalizes the encounter and makes them realize their own accountability.

Whenever possible, get to know the teachers and principals at nearby schools. In some cases, they will be able to help you by offering specific strategies for dealing with kids who are causing problems. In any case, it can be an enormous influence if you are able to say to a misbehaving tween or teen, "What do you think Ms. Johnson would say if I told her you were behaving like that?" He or she will be shocked that you actually know Ms. Johnson, but it can make a difference in his or her behavior!

As much as possible, deal with teens one-on-one. If you reprimand a teen in front of his or her friends, he or she will not react well. Teens need to maintain their chosen image in front of their peers, so when you challenge them, you can make them look bad in front of friends. The likely result will be even more poor choices, as they bluster and posture to regain their image. When you are talking to a teen, maintain eye contact, and ask him or her to confirm that he or she understands what you are saying. Avoid sounding accusatory ("you did this") and instead focus on the results of the action. ("My concern is that someone will get hurt if the shoving and horseplay continue.")

When you can, ask teens to engage in identifying potential options for behavior and its consequences. You can assist them in considering the pros and cons of each of those options. Not only can this lead to a resolution of the problem, it also gives the brain a workout that develops reasoning and decision-making skills for the future. Teens work best in a structure of empowerment, in which the adults around them offer warmth and concern, set limits, and honor their autonomy.

Promote the positive. Not only is it a good idea to put requests for teens into positive language (saying, for example, "Please walk" instead of "Don't run"), but in general they respond better to positive reasons to do something rather than negative reasons not to do it. In his book *Brainstorm*, Dr. Daniel Siegel points out the case of public health efforts to reduce teen smoking. The negative strategies of attempting to frighten teens away from smoking by showing them pictures of blackened lungs and images of graveyards had no effect on whether teens started or continued to smoke. On the other hand, when teens were told that tobacco company executives were trying to manipulate and brainwash teens by making smoking sound attractive in order to get them hooked and have their money for life, the rate of teen smoking dropped (Siegel 2013, 80).

If you do have to ask a teen to leave the library, make it for a specific period of time. This can be for as little as 30 minutes or an hour, if you think a teen just needs some time and space to cool off, or it can be for as long as a week or a month, if there has been an ongoing and particularly serious problem. Most often, you will ask a teen to leave for the rest of the day. No matter how long the teen has been gone, make it clear that the next time he or she comes to the library will be a clean slate. Be positive and optimistic that on this occasion the teen will be able to start over fresh and exhibit positive behaviors. When this teen does return, greet him or her with a smile and don't make references to the previous bad behavior. Assume that everything will be fine; you will be amazed at how often it is!

If a situation is so serious that you must mandate a longer time period away from the library, make a clear set of criteria for the teen's return. This may include something like, "You cannot come back to the library for two weeks. And before you come back, I will need to meet with you and a parent, so we can come to an understanding about what acceptable behavior in the library is."

Above all, deal with behaviors, not personalities. It is not a teen who is the problem, but rather the specific choice about how to behave that she has just made.

DEALING WITH GROUPS OF TEENS

During the adolescent years, the teen's world begins to center more around friends than around family. This is a normal part of adolescent development and helps teens explore their new sense of identity. Having friends allows teens to see different sets of family values and beliefs and to try out their own growing sense of morality. Peer groups enable teens to see how they are both different from and the same as their parents.

At the same time, groups of teenagers in the library can be intimidating and alarming to other library users, particularly if the teens are being noisy, rowdy, or disruptive. But there are ways to deal with groups of teens in the library.

First, if the same teens are in your library every day, make a point of observing them. It should become fairly obvious who is the leader (or leaders) of the group. One way to tell is to watch where the noise level is—if it moves around, but the same person is in every loud group, there's the person you want to watch.

Second, learn that person's name. Just knowing the name is a start, but if at all possible, get to know that kid on a personal level.

Third, when things get wild and crazy, start by pulling that person aside for a conversation. Even if you haven't identified a "leader," start by pulling just one teen aside for the initial conversation. Teens are much more likely to posture and become aggressive if you approach them in front of their peers, so if at all possible, move yourself and your troublemaker to a place in the library where you are not on view to the group, although you should still be in a public space. Then just talk. Don't start with accusations; rather, ask something like, "What do you think is going on today? It seems really noisy." Let him or her tell you what is happening. It might be that everyone is keyed up because of something that happened at school, or in the community, and the kids really just needed to be able to process it together. It might be that it is the end of the school year, and they're just so antsy they can hardly sit still.

Fourth, engage the teen in a discussion about what can be done about the situation. Keep your remarks as positive as possible, but point out the problems as you see them: "I'm really happy that you and your friends have come to the library today, and that you like hanging out here. But today the noise level has gotten so bad that other groups in the library can't study or even think. I hope that you can go back and convince everyone else that they need to settle down, because I'd like you to be able to stay in the library. But if you don't think that can happen, I'm going to need to ask all of you to leave for the rest of the day. What do you think? Can you get the noise levels down?"

When you are having this conversation, whether it is about a group's activities or one person's misbehavior, keep to your point, and don't let the teen distract you. It's all right for you to say the same thing over and over again. If you allow the teen to hijack the conversation and bring in all kinds of extraneous issues, then the teen wins: he or she has succeeded in not making a choice about his or her behavior.

DISTRACTING VERSUS DANGEROUS BEHAVIOR

One of the best ways to deal with teen behavior in the library is to make a clear distinction in your own mind between *distracting* behaviors and *dangerous* behaviors. By far the majority of teen behaviors that many adults object to are distracting behaviors. They are irritating to adults, but they aren't really serious problems. Examples include teens who are socializing loudly with one another, teens who move the furniture around, teens who hang out in groups around the computers, teens who are eating and drinking in nondesignated spaces, teens who are making out in the corner, and teens who are running, gently shoving one another, or sitting in the aisles. All of these behaviors may be problematic, but none is a dangerous behavior.

Dangerous behaviors are those in which serious harm may be done to another person or to library property. Possession of weapons or illegal substances, verbal or physical bullying, or assault are dangerous behaviors. But it is important to distinguish between actual assault—intentional and unwanted touching or striking of another—and the kinds of normal horseplay that teens engage in—hugging, mock fighting, and so on. It is usually easy to tell them apart, but in case of doubt, it is the victim who has the last word on whether he or she was assaulted.

Some staff members may have differing views on whether a particular behavior is dangerous or merely distracting. Say, for example, you notice an unusual odor and discover that a teen has lit a stick of incense in the library (true story!). One staff member may regard that as dangerous behavior, because fire was involved. Another might see that the lighter is no longer in evidence and the incense isn't likely to set anything on fire and realize that the teen was merely having one of those immature moments. Regarding this as dangerous behavior might involve anything from calling the police or fire department or the teen's parents to kicking him or her out of the library for a time. Regarding this as distracting behavior, on the other hand, would indicate a more low-key approach: inviting the teen outside the building to dispose of the incense stick safely and having a conversation about whether he or she really thought that lighting incense in the library was appropriate. Chances are, the teen will sheepishly admit that it was stupid and agree not to do it again. Remember, even smart, savvy teens have their immature moments, and if showing off for peers is involved, anything can happen!

Generally speaking, it is wise to assume the best. If you assume that a teen who is engaging in distracting behavior is immature, not malicious, life will go more easily for both of you. Often the kinds of stupid things teens do is a result of their natural tendency toward experimentation and innovation. If possible, honor that tendency. As Dr. Daniel Siegel (2013, 80) puts it, "Honoring does not mean setting no limits. It means acknowledging the intention behind the actions." Having a conversation with a teen who is engaging in distracting behaviors can enable us, as adults, to help him or her see that there might be another more appropriate way to achieve his or her goal—of making a particular point, impressing a peer, or whatever it is.

Dangerous behaviors, on the other hand, must be dealt with swiftly and firmly. Failing to deal with dangerous situations may cause teens to feel that coming to the library is harmful to them, not a positive factor. Teens and other library users need to know that the library is as safe a place as any public place can be.

Hungry, Angry, Lonely, Tired (HALT)

Various chemical dependency and recovery programs, including Alcoholics Anonymous, use the acronym HALT as a tool for people to recognize the states that might trigger a relapse or other inappropriate behavior. It is a tool that can be very useful in dealing with teens (and adults!) in the library. So when faced with distracting behaviors on the part of teens, it can be helpful to ask ourselves if they are:

- *Hungry*. Teen bodies are still growing, and they often grow in spurts. Especially if they come to the library directly after school, they may be genuinely hungry. If your library does not allow food in the building, you may experience one of two problems: either teens will sneak food into the building, or they will exhibit signs of hunger: headache, irritability, lack of concentration. Encouraging teens to go get a snack and then come back can be helpful.
- *Angry*. We all experience anger at times in response to the stresses in our lives. As adults, we get angry with friends and family over issues large and small, or we get stressed by our commute, or not having enough time to do everything we want to do, or paying bills. Teens likewise have stresses that can bring on anger: homework, sports, relationships, and even the way they see their own bodies in comparison to others'. Teens are subjected to many rules in our society: rules at home, at school, in their city, and sometimes these rules can conflict with one another, causing more frustration. For example, they're supposed to get all their homework done, but they're also expected to participate in extra-curricular activities, do chores at home, maybe have a job or go to church, and then they're told that they should go to bed earlier.

  In addition, gender and culture play a part in anger and how teens express it. In Western culture, for example, women are not supposed to express anger—although they are encouraged to talk about their feelings. Men, on the other hand, are allowed to externalize anger but are expected to keep their feelings inside. Some cultures that are male-dominated lead their young men to have disrespect for women, especially those in power, and most library staff is female.

  Teens who are angry may need a time out, to go outside and do something to burn off their negative energy, like run around the building.
- *Lonely*. We can all feel lonely, even if we are in the midst of many other people. Because of their developmental stage, all teens, at one time or another, feel disconnected from their family, their peers, and society. This loneliness may cause them to act in ways that are distracting and disruptive. There are many strategies for dealing with lonely teens, including getting them involved in programs and volunteer activities.

- *Tired*. As we discussed in Chapter 1, most teens are chronically sleep-deprived. By the time they get to the library, they have probably already gotten up too early, spent a full day in classes, possibly done an activity like sports or music, and probably had some sort of commute. Of course they're tired and irritable! If these teens are stuck at the library waiting for a ride, they are going to cause problems. If possible, try to have some spots in the library where they can just relax in comfortable chairs, listen to their music or watch a video, and just generally take it easy for a little while.

You may not be able to do much to alleviate any of these conditions. However, just being aware of the possibilities will make you less likely to overreact to the behavior and more likely to be able to have a compassionate response. Such a response will serve both you and the teen better in the long run.

TEEN PARTICIPATION IN PROGRAMS AND SERVICES

One of the best ways to develop good, positive relationships with teens in the library is to involve them. Providing teens with opportunities to be active participants in library decision-making empowers teens. It gives them ways to form relationships with adult library workers and with each other and to use their time and opportunities to demonstrate—and expand—their own skills. Clearly, all of these factors fit right into the developmental assets and the concept of connected learning that we discussed in Chapter 1.

Some libraries have formal teen advisory boards. These may come in many different forms, but their main purpose is to involve teens in responsible action and significant decision-making in their library. A good teen advisory board will have adult guidance and support, but it will not be dominated by adults. Teens will have the opportunity to provide input into library programs and materials and to participate in decisions on matters that affect them. Libraries that use teen advisory boards often find, for example, that their teen programs have better attendance because the teen advisers not only suggest programs of interest to themselves but they also encourage their friends and peers to attend.

Some libraries have active teen volunteer programs, either instead of or in addition to an advisory board. Many high schools today require service learning hours, and volunteering at the library may be one way to meet that requirement. Other libraries utilize the expertise of the teens who are employed there as pages or shelvers and still others take advantage of the existence of a local youth board that advises the city council or other governing body. The point to remember is that everything a library does for and with teens—collections, programs, facilities, services—can benefit from teen input. Not only do these types of opportunities give teens valuable experience and validation, they serve to introduce the rest of the library staff and members of the community to teens who are working positively to make the world a better place. Many teens who start as volunteers or members of teen advisory boards go on to become library workers themselves, and all of them have the potential to be great ambassadors for the library in the wider world.

When you do invite teen input, formally or informally, do them the courtesy of letting them know the result. If a teen suggests that the library buy a particular book, either inform the teen that it has been purchased, or let him or her know why the library decided not to buy it. If teens suggest programs, follow up with them by telling them which programs will be implemented and why.

If you do not have a teen advisory board, you can start by involving the teens who regularly use your library. Ask them to give you suggestions for materials or to help you brainstorm program ideas. This kind of informal teen participation may eventually evolve into a formal teen advisory board, but even if it doesn't, you are getting valuable input.

CONCLUSION

Having positive interactions with teens in the library isn't as complicated or mysterious as it sometimes appears. Teenagers are people—they just happen to be people who are going through a whole lot of changes in their bodies, minds, and emotions, and those changes clearly affect the way they act and react in various situations. As a library worker, you will have more positive interactions with teens if you bear in mind that you are the adult. This doesn't mean that you should be overbearing, but it does mean that you have the ability to control your emotions in ways that teens don't, and therefore you have the responsibility to keep any situation from getting out of control. Keep in mind the reasons that teens act the way they do, treat them with respect and maintain your own sense of dignity and authority, and you will be able to deal successfully with any issue that comes up in the library.

REFERENCES

APA. 2002. "Developing Adolescents: A Resource for Professionals." Available at: http://www.apa.org/pi/families/resources/develop.pdf.

Parry, Vivienne. March 2, 2005. "It's Not Just the Hormones." *The Guardian*. Available at: https://www.theguardian.com/science/2005/mar/03/1.

Siegel, Daniel. 2013. *Brainstorm: The Power and Purpose of the Teenage Brain*. New York: JeremyTarcher/Penguin.

CHAPTER 3

Teen Collections

Most children stay in the children's room when they come to the library, and most adults never venture out of the adult department, unless they are parents of small children. Teens, on the other hand, often freely use the entire library, both for their recreational and for their informational needs. Teens are neither children nor adults, but they have characteristics of both. This means that there really is no such thing as a single, small teen collection, but rather teens may want or need materials that may be found in every part of the library. When helping teens with both informational and recreational needs, it is a good idea to consider materials from the whole library.

YOUNG ADULT LITERATURE

Young adult (YA) literature is a relatively new concept, just as "teenager" is a relatively new concept. Both ideas really began to flourish in the mid-twentieth century, when adolescents began to stay in school longer and live at home until they were in their late teens. The first YA books were primarily "problem novels"—realistic fiction that focused on the particular issues of adolescence, including coming of age, dealing with sex, alcohol, drugs, and family situations, and so on. As Marc Aronson (2001, 8) says that what those problem novels provided to readers was to make "the shock of recognition—'Hey, I am not alone, other people have felt what I feel'—the heart of YA fiction." Today, the field of young adult literature has expanded to include a vast array of fiction and nonfiction and cover every subject, genre, theme, and topic imaginable. In truth, the only thing that makes a book a "YA book" is the fact that its publisher has designated it for readers between the ages of, roughly, 12 and 18.

Teens do, of course, read books that are specifically marketed to teens, but they also read books that are written for adults, and many still read books that are "children's" books, especially if the author is a favorite from their own childhood reading. So YA or teen collections in libraries can vary widely, depending on the budget, philosophy, and demographics of the library.

COLLECTIONS FOR TEENS

What is in the teen collection at any particular library will be influenced by the library's collection development policy. Almost all libraries have a collection development policy, and the teen collection will fit within the larger policy. If the library collects only popular materials—bestsellers, genre fiction, feature film DVDs, popular music CDs, and so on—then the YA collection will probably be similar. Some public libraries heavily support the curriculum of local schools, buying textbooks and other materials that focus on common assignments. Others leave curriculum support to the schools and focus their nonfiction collections on popular materials.

Knowing what your library collects, and why, can help you find materials to serve teens. For example, one library might focus recreational reading and personal growth materials, rather than on curriculum support. That library would be likely to collect broadly and deeply in many areas that can and do serve as curriculum support, but these items would not be shelved in the teen area. Another library, in contrast, might have a policy that states its intention to collect nonfiction titles that include both popular, high interest titles and those that supplement the curriculum of the local schools. That library might shelve the curriculum items separately, or interfile them with adult or children's nonfiction.

The teen department may also collect materials or formats that are not ordinarily collected by the library. To meet the needs for popular materials for teens, for example, it may be reasonable to collect console games, anime, manga and graphic novels, and other formats that may or may not be common in the children's or adult areas.

TEEN INPUT

Teens often have very definite ideas about what they are interested in. The best way to find out what kinds of materials they want in the library is to listen to them. If the library has a teen advisory group, that can be very helpful, but it is also important to listen carefully to the teens who are using the library regularly: What kinds of materials are they requesting? In what formats? What are they reading, listening to, or watching while in the library? What are they carrying around with them? Having a suggestion box or some other easily accessible way for teens to suggest new titles is a good way to find out what they want.

Teens are often quite absorbed with popular culture: the latest television shows, movies, actors, singers, YouTube sensations, and so on. If library staff consistently fails to provide teens with a variety of options that are related to their specific interests, they will come to regard libraries as worthless and obsolete, so it is worthwhile to make some attempts to keep up with the latest celebrities and trends. One way to do this is to identify one or two magazines to read regularly, like *People*, *Teen Vogue*, or *Entertainment Weekly*. Or find some websites that do the same thing; *Teen Vogue*, *E! Online*, and *TMZ* are examples. A great source for all things pop culture for girls is *Rookie Magazine*, an online magazine that has also produced several "yearbooks" containing compilations of articles, interviews, photographs, and stories from the website. Even if someone else in the library does the materials selection, becoming familiar with some of the popular culture topics of interest to teens will help you in answering requests from teens and in suggesting materials to the person in the library who does selection.

The YA publishing world has exploded in the past 20 years, with thousands of books being published for teens each year. It is impossible to keep up with all of them, but it is a good idea to have some idea of what the most popular and the most critically acclaimed books are. The Young Adult Library Services Association (YALSA) is a good resource here. Every year YALSA members compile lists of the best books, videos, and audiobooks for teens, and YALSA honors some with awards, such as the Printz Award for best book written for teens, the Morris Award for best debut work, and the Excellence in Nonfiction Award. The YALSA booklists and awards page (http://www.ala.org/yalsa/bookawards/booklists/members) is an extremely valuable resource for finding out about the cream of the crop for teen materials. The lists go back, in some cases, 15 years, and some of the lists, like Best Fiction for Young Adults and Quick Picks for Reluctant Young Adult Read-er*s*, include lists of the currently nominated titles, so you can find out what's new and what's hot.

TRANSLITERACY

"Transliteracy" is a relatively new term in the library world. It refers to the ability to read, write, and interact across a range of platforms, tools, and media. Many—even most—teens today are operating in the transliteracy mode. Teens often just go about things differently from adults, and that can include the ways they "read": print books, graphic novels and other sequential art, audiobooks, films, games, and so on. They move from one to another seamlessly, and our collections and our readers' advisory both need to acknowledge this range.

To be transliterate ourselves, we need to be able to identify the right format for the information that the person in front of us needs right now. Sometimes it may be a book, sometimes a website, sometimes an audiobook or podcast, sometimes a video, and so on. Having an awareness of various sources can be of great help in responding to both reference and readers' advisory queries.

Graphic Novels

Some materials, like graphic novels, require us to use multiple literacies. As Francisca Goldsmith (2009, 5) says, "The text [of graphic novels] requires traditional decoding skills, while the images require the reader to interpret facial and body language as well as the use of white space and shading, and be oriented to the flow of panels as they carry the narrative forward." She goes on to point out that the reader must have the ability to "apprehend word and image synchronically."

In addition to the growing body of graphic novels, many teens also enjoy reading traditional Japanese-style graphic novels, called *manga*. More and more manga is being published in English, and it requires yet another decoding skill, as it is typically published to mimic the Japanese-style of printing, with pages running from right to left instead of left to right.

This is a different style of reading from traditional text reading, and it takes practice to learn how to do it. But as more and more graphic novels are being published, today's young people are learning that skill at earlier and earlier ages. Unlike picture books, where the pictures (usually) illustrate text content, in graphic novels, the illustrations actually convey important information that the reader needs to know in order to follow the story. Image and text must be interpreted together. If you just read the text, or just look at the pictures, you are going to miss an important part of the book. In addition, action occurs between frames, so the reader must actively engage in deducing what has happened: What does it mean, for example, when two characters are looking at one another in one frame, but back-to-back in the next?

Many adults—including librarians—subscribe to one or more of these myths about graphic novels:

> **Myth 1. Graphic novels are a genre.** No, graphic novels are a format. A graphic novel may be in any genre—mystery, science fiction, realistic fiction, nonfiction (yes, we still call them graphic "novels" even if they are nonfiction!).
>
> **Myth 2. Graphic novels are easier to read, so we should recommend them to reluctant readers.** While some reluctant readers may prefer a graphic format, it is by no means a certainty. As noted earlier, reading graphic novels is a different type of reading, one that involves decoding both words and pictures simultaneously. While some struggling readers may find that the cues given by the pictures help them decode the words, others may just find the whole prospect overwhelming.
>
> **Myth 3. Graphic novels are the same as comic books.** Graphic novels are narratives presented in a sequential art format. Comic books may contain sequential art narratives, but they are more like magazines, in that they are ephemeral. In the library world, we tend to call anything a graphic novel if it is bound like a book; this could include multiple issues of a comic book that are bound together as one. Purists would not consider that a graphic novel, but for the purposes of cataloging, shelving, and readers' advisory in the library, it would be considered a graphic novel.
>
> **Myth 4. All graphic novels are about superheroes.** Graphic novels can be about anything.
>
> **Myth 5. Only teens read graphic novels.** There are graphic novels for all age ranges. In the past few years, several graphic novels for children have won both Newbery and Caldecott Awards. There are some popular and critically acclaimed graphic novels for adults, like Roz Chast's *Can't We Talk about Something More Pleasant?*, that would have little appeal for teens because it is about dealing with aging parents.
>
> **Myth 6. All teens like graphic novels.** Teens have their own unique tastes. As with any type of reading, you need to listen to teens and find out what their specific

interests are. Do they like manga? Do they want realistic fiction or do they prefer memoir? Are they more interested in character or plot? What are their visual preferences: full-color or two-color? Representational or fantastical/abstract?

Audiobooks

Some teens like to "read with their ears" by listening to audiobooks. A large percentage of new young adult fiction and nonfiction is now also published in audiobook format. Although libraries may maintain collections of audiobooks on CD, most teens prefer listening to them on their smartphones and mobile devices. Having downloadable audiobooks gives teens another way to approach both pleasure reading and assigned reading. As Mary Burkey (2012, 77) says, "As the very definitions of 'reading' and 'book' are rewritten, new digital formats allow a reinterpretation of literacy. The ability to shift seamlessly from image to text to sound will be part of every young person's transliterate education."

DIVERSITY

Another challenge can be finding books and other materials that match the diversity of the community—or even materials that provide windows for local teens into diverse cultures. At various times, teens want to read about "people just like me" and about those whose lives they see as exotic and different. What those two extremes will look like will depend, naturally, on what the individuals themselves are like. Marc Aronson (2001, 14) points out that in "the Jewish, black, and Hispanic high school I went to . . . there was nothing more exotic than Irish Catholics."

In June 2013, Lee and Low Books published an article titled "Why Hasn't the Number of Multicultural Books Increased in 18 Years?" Using statistics from the U.S. census and the Cooperative Children's Book Center, Lee and Low demonstrated that while 37 percent of the U.S. population are people of color, only 10 percent of the roughly 3,500 children's (including YA) books that are published each year contain characters of color. What's more, in 2015, 60 percent of the books published about people of color were created by people outside of those cultures (Low 2013). Lee and Low updates the statistics each year.

A good first stop in the search for diverse literature is the We Need Diverse Books website (http://www.weneeddiversebooks.org). We Need Diverse Books is, in their words, "a grassroots organization of children's book lovers that advocates essential changes in the publishing industry to produce and promote literature that reflects and honors the lives of all young people." The website contains a wealth of resources for librarians and others who are looking for books about diverse cultures, ethnicities, sexual identities, genders, disabilities, and more. They link to review sources and maintain a blog to discuss current issues and new books.

As Jamie Campbell Naidoo (2014) points out in a white paper written for the Association for Library Service to Children (ALSC), "By including diversity in its programs and collections, the library has the potential for helping children make cross-cultural connections and develop the skills necessary to function in a culturally pluralistic society."

It is easy to fall into the trap of deciding that you do not need to buy any materials about a particular ethnic group because no one in your community fits that particular profile. But consider this story from author Matt de la Peña in his 2016 Newbery Medal acceptance speech:

> At one of the big national conferences, a librarian approached me outside an event space and excitedly introduced herself. "I want you to know," she told me, "that I really like your books. I mean, we don't have those kinds of kids at our school, so we don't stock many of them, but I want you to know how much I appreciate your work."
>
> "No, I totally get it, ma'am," I said. "Out of curiosity, though, how many wizards do you have at your school?"

SELECTION RESOURCES

Most libraries use standard selection tools. Many of these, like *Booklist, School Library Journal, Publishers Weekly*, and *Library Journal*, contain reviews for teen materials as well as reviews for adult and/or children's materials. The *Voice of Youth Advocates (VOYA)* magazine focuses specifically on YA literature and reading with over 350 book reviews in each issue. But even these journals and websites review only a fraction of the materials in which teens may be interested. It can sometimes be a challenge, for example, to find good reviews of anime and manga, although the standard review sources are beginning to include more reviews of graphic novels and graphic nonfiction.

Electronic discussion lists that can point you toward new titles in various genres. YALSA-BK is an active list on which new books for teens are frequently discussed. GN4LIB does the same for graphic novels. Amazon's teen page contains reviews by professional reviewers as well as by teen readers. Goodreads and Library Thing have reviews of teen books by both adult and teen readers.

Library workers can also sign up for NetGalley (www.netgalley.com) and Edelweiss (edelweiss.abovethetreeline.com). These are sites where publishers offer electronic "galleys" (prepublished books). You can request access to specific books in exchange for offering reviews. Even just browsing these sites can give you a good idea of what is coming out soon, and what the hottest books and trends are. Edelweiss includes complete publisher catalogs and detailed information about the publisher's plans for marketing individual books.

Another tip on keeping up with teen interests is to explore magazines. Magazines are often very popular with teens, especially boys. Explore the magazine section at a large bookstore and watch to see which magazines teens pick up. Or go to a hobby store, music store, or video game store to find out what is out there and what kinds of magazines the teens in your library might enjoy. Watch to see which magazines in the library's collection they read and look for similar ones.

READERS' ADVISORY

Readers' advisory is generally defined as helping a library user find recreational reading (or viewing, or listening), as opposed to helping with informational needs, such as homework or personal growth questions. It can be a challenge, especially with teens, who can sometimes find it difficult to express exactly what they are looking for. However, readers' advisory inquiries can be great opportunities to connect with teens; if you recommend a book that a teen loves, you will gain credibility. Even if your suggestions aren't successful, if you take teens seriously and treat their requests with respect they will be more likely to come back in the future—and they may start making recommendations to you!

Questions

If a teen approaches to ask for help in finding a book, you're off to a good start. However, many teens are not even aware that library staff can help them to find recreational materials, so be alert to signals that a teen is looking for something to read (or to watch or listen to). If a teen is wandering around the stacks, picking up books occasionally or talking about books with a friend, consider asking:

- What's a book you've read recently and really liked (or hated)?
- What did you like (hate) about it?
- Do you like fiction or nonfiction? (If they're not sure, try saying made-up stories or true stories.)
- Do you have a favorite author?
- Do you like mysteries? (Science fiction? Fantasy? School stories? Vampire books? Sports? Romance?)
- Do you care about the age or gender or culture of the characters?
- Do you like scary books? (Funny books? Sad books? Adventure books?)
- What are your favorite TV shows?
- What movies do you like?
- What kinds of music do you listen to?
- What kinds of afterschool activities are you involved in?

Try not to overwhelm the teen with these questions, though. The idea is to get a conversation going, so that you can start thinking about books that might meet the teen's interests. Be aware of the teen's reactions during this conversation. Try to pick up on expressions of interest, but match your level of energy with theirs so that you don't scare them away.

Appeal Factors

Readers look for different things in a book, so it's not enough to focus simply on what a book is "about." Some readers care more about characters than plot. Some people prefer to read fast-paced page-turners; others want a slower pace. Some love descriptions of people and places; others want lots of dialogue to move the story along quickly. Some want a simple, straightforward story, while others relish a complex multilayered read. And some want all of these things, just at different times.

Teens, unlike adults, are often still unformed in their reading choices. They are much more likely to read across genres and styles than adults are, and more likely to take a chance on something new and different. They may also not yet have the skills to decode a book's content quickly and easily, by looking at the cover illustration, the jacket blurbs, and so on. These are skills that librarians can model for teens in sharing books.

Some things one is well to avoid saying with teens. A teen is really not interested in the fact that this was your favorite book when you were a teenager. To a teen that just says the book is old. And unless they know you really well, most teens don't care that it is your son or daughter's favorite book, either. On the other hand, if a celebrity they like has mentioned the book, it could stir interest. Also, avoid making generalizations like "everyone should read this." This particular teen in front of you isn't "everyone" and doesn't want to be lumped with everyone.

Suggest several titles. Let teens know that these are just suggestions, and that they should feel free to take one or more but that they are under no obligation to take any of them. You can ask them to let you know later if they liked any of the books, but then walk away and give them time to look at the items you've suggested. And don't be hurt if they just leave the entire stack of books on the table.

Resources for Readers' Advisory

So how do you find something to recommend, especially if you don't read a lot of teen literature? Start with the selection resources previously mentioned. There's no real substitute for reading widely, but there are many resources to help you find books for teens. Don't forget that many teens read adult literature as much as or more than they read teen literature, and many teens are also still reading, at least occasionally, from the children's section.

You can start with your library's catalog. Fortunately, most fiction now includes subject headings, so if a teen is interested in reading books that feature a particular topic, like knitting or motorcycles, you can just enter the topic plus the word "fiction" into your online catalog to get some titles.

Next, see what kinds of lists your library has already created. Most libraries have online booklists, as well as paper ones, geared to specific topics, and most libraries also create "read-alike" lists of books to suggest to teens who have liked a particular popular book, like *Twilight* or *The Hunger Games*. To find these lists, just do a quick web search using the title of a book and the word "read-alikes"; there will be links to libraries as well as other sites that have prepared these booklists.

Some useful websites and blogs that contain teen booklists and book reviews are:

- Adult Books 4 Teens (http://www.slj.com/category/collection-development/adult-books-for-teens/). Reviews of new books that were published for adults but have appeal for teens. A "best of the year" list is published in December.
- Epic Reads (http://www.epicreads.com/books/) is a great place to keep up on new YA books. The site includes information about new and upcoming books, plus lots of fun things like quizzes, booklists, read-alikes, book trailers, and more.
- The Hub (http://www.yalsa.ala.org/thehub/) is YALSA's Teen Literature blog. It contains reviews and analysis, "read-alikes" lists, and much more.
- No Flying, No Tights (http://noflyingnotights.com) is a graphic novel review site, featuring reviews from librarians of graphic novels for children, teens, and adults. They review only graphic novels that are available to libraries via standard library book jobbers, such as Baker & Taylor, Ingram, and Follett. They also have staff picks for various ages, and lists of "Must Haves" and "Classic Fantastic."
- Stacked (http://stackedbooks.org) is a blog by a YA librarian and former YA librarian that does a good job keeping up to date on YA books and providing in-depth looks at YA literature. One especially nice feature is frequent lists of upcoming debut novels.
- Someday My Printz Will Come (http://blogs.slj.com/printzblog/) is *School Library Journal*'s blog about books that are eligible for the Printz Award, YALSA's top award

for teen books. The blog is primarily active during the three to four months leading up to each year's award announcements, which occur in January or February. The articles are generally very thoughtful and deep, and the comments section is lively and well worth reading.

- Teen Services Underground's Booklists (http://www.teenservicesunderground.com/features/booklists/). Booklists are contributed by librarians who work with teens. The website also includes a section with tips and techniques for doing readers' advisory with teens.

- YALSA's Book Awards and Booklists (http://www.ala.org/yalsa/bookawards/booklists/members). Every year YALSA members create a number of book and media lists and select titles for awards. Some are selected lists, like Best Fiction for Young Adults, Quick Picks for Reluctant Readers, Great Graphic Novels, and Amazing Audiobooks. Others are awards, like the Michael L. Printz Award, the Excellence in Nonfiction for Young Adults Award, the Morris Award for a debut book, and the Odyssey Award for an audiobook. The Alex Award selects 10 adult books with teen appeal. The Nonfiction and Alex Awards also include lists of other books that didn't make the final cut but were seriously considered. Popular Paperbacks creates themed lists of books that are popular with teens and currently available in paperback. These lists are essential for anyone selecting teen materials or doing readers' advisory with teens.

Your library may subscribe to some readers' advisory databases; it is worthwhile to explore these and learn how to use them effectively. EBSCO's NoveList database, Book-Browse, and Booklist Online all allow searching by various settings, genres, and subjects.

BOOKTALKING

Booktalking is simply a way of promoting a library collection by enticing a reader into picking up a book (or video or magazine or audio). A booktalk is essentially a sales pitch. Booktalks are often done informally in the stacks or one-on-one, but they can also be done in a formal setting, for example, in a classroom or library meeting room full of teens. Booktalks can be aimed at teens themselves or at parents, teachers, and library staffers. Booktalks can be a few seconds long—not much more than a tag line—or they can be up to several minutes long. The key thing is to sell the book—not give a review or criticism of it and not to describe it in exhausting detail.

Each booktalker has his or her own way of doing booktalks, but there are some general types. Think about a booktalk as a movie trailer or the blurb on the back of a paperback: something to give you an idea of the plot, the characters, the setting, but not so much that it spoils the surprise of actually reading the book.

Informal Booktalks

An informal booktalk is usually just a sentence or two, something that you can share with someone as you are standing together in the library. The key is to give an idea of the style or subject of the book and to tantalize the reader into wanting more. For example:

- Sig is alone in a remote cabin with the dead body of his father when a man shows up demanding the gold that he says Sig's father owes him. (*Revolver*, by Marcus Sedgwick)

- This one is about a boy with mad cow disease who goes on a road trip with a dwarf, a yard gnome, and an angel, to try to save the world. (*Going Bovine*, by Libba Bray)
- This is a retelling of the Rumpelstiltskin story, set in an 18th-century woolen mill. (A *Curse Dark as Gold*, by Elizabeth Bunce)
- Here's one about mermaids, curses, history, and murder. (*Monstrous Beauty*, by Elizabeth Fama)
- "Audrey, Wait" is the hit new breakup song. Audrey is the real girl it was written about, and she's not thrilled about being famous for dumping a rock star. (*Audrey, Wait*, by Robin Benway)

Nonfiction can be presented in the same way:

- Did you know that there were 13 women pilots who went through all the same training as the original astronauts, and in most cases they did better on the tests than the men did—but they weren't allowed to be astronauts? (*Almost Astronauts*, by Tanya Lee Stone)
- Have you ever watched *Bones*? This book is about some real-life forensic anthropologists and what they found in the Chesapeake Bay area. (*Written in Bone*, by Sally M. Walker)
- You might not know that building the first atomic bomb during World War II had incidents that were as exciting as an action-adventure movie—like the Norwegian commandos who skied in at night to blow up a Nazi heavy-water plant. (*Bomb: The Race to Build—and Steal—the World's Most Dangerous Weapon*, by Steve Sheinkin)
- What happens when an 8th-grade geek girl decides to follow the advice of a 1950s popularity handbook? Find out in *Popular*, a memoir by Maya Van Wagenen.

Formal Booktalks

Formal booktalks are usually longer and give some more detail. They may mimic the mood or tone of the book: slow and creepy for a scary book like *The Monstrumologist*, by Rick Yancey, or zany and a little strange for a quirky book like *Going Bovine*. They may focus on the plot, telling just enough of the story to get the listeners interested but stopping at a cliffhanger point. They may focus on the characters, especially the main character.

You can booktalk anything, but some books make better booktalks than others. Fast-paced, suspenseful books allow you to set up a situation and leave the listener wanting to know what happens next. Nonfiction books often make great booktalks because you can share a little-known fact or even turn it into a story. Books about the supernatural work well because you can focus on the way the supernatural provides an unusual twist to the story, which could be a love story, an adventure story, or just about anything else. Funny books allow you to tell a funny story and get them hooked that way. Books with unusual formats—letters, e-mails, instant messages, scripts, poems—can often be intriguing in themselves, no matter the plot. You don't have to booktalk only new books, either. Booktalks are a great way to get older books to move.

How to Get Started

Everyone who booktalks eventually develops his or her own style. But here are a few things to keep in mind:

- Don't give away the ending.
- Don't oversell the book—gushing doesn't work.
- Don't just give a plot summary.
- Keep description to a minimum.
- Don't tell every detail of the story, just enough to get them intrigued.
- Keep it short.

To start a booktalk, think about the books you have read recently and want to share with others. What was special or unique about them? What got you interested? Here are a few ways you can start:

- With a character. Give the audience an idea of who this character is (good or bad).
- With a question. This gets your audience thinking about how they would answer it.
- With an action. This jumps the audience right into the middle of the story.
- With a shared experience. This is something in the book that the audience may also have experienced, felt, seen, or said. It might also be a question, like "Have you ever gone on a road trip?" that can be a lead in to a book about a particular road trip.
- With a shocker. This shouldn't be the ending, but it could be some other shocking incident in the book.

The middle of the booktalk should tell just enough to get the audience interested, but not so much that they get bored.

The last line of the booktalk should be memorable—a question the audience wants answered, or a cliffhanger that leads them to ask for more. Sometimes it works well to use the title of the book in the last line, but don't force it. It's just a good way to get the audience to remember the book you're talking about.

Some booktalkers like to use the first-person booktalk. So many books for teens are written in first person, and it is an easy step to do the booktalk in the voice of the main character. These kinds of booktalks can be very effective, especially if you're a good actor and you really convey the voice of the character. On the other hand, they can fall flat or cause giggling in the audience if you are so far removed from the character that they can't connect.

Why Booktalk?

Booktalking can help you increase your library's circulation. It promotes the library as a place where teens can find books to read for fun. It allows you to be creative and have fun, while promoting the collection. And it gives you a chance to build relationships with teens and others.

You may never have an opportunity to do a program of booktalks. But learning and practicing booktalking skills is valuable anyway. It gives you confidence in sharing books with others, so you're not standing there, stumbling and saying, "Oh, you'll love this book; it's, um, about a girl, and, uh, she's in high school, and she has this friend who died, and, oh, yeah, her father is an alcoholic and then this guy shows up . . ."

As you read a new book, think about how you might booktalk it. You can practice by writing short summaries of the books you read and keeping them—in a journal, in a spreadsheet, or in an online book tracking site like Goodreads or Library Thing. After you've had some practice, give a short booktalk to your spouse, your child, or a colleague. Once you've done it a few times, go ahead—try it on a library user who is looking for a

good book to read. It is not necessary for every library worker to be a booktalking professional, but learning something about the techniques is a good way to focus your attention
on presenting books and other materials in an appealing light.

Booktalking is just one way to connect teens with books. Having a collection that
appeals to teens and meets their needs is the first step. Then find ways to market that collection, both formally and informally. Booktalking can be an effective part of this, but so
can other forms of marketing, like displays, booklists, and video book trailers.

BOOK TRAILERS

A newer version of the booktalk is the book trailer. These are like movie trailers, only
they are for books. Many publishers post professional book trailers on their websites, but
fans create them as well. Creating a book trailer is a popular exercise in school libraries,
as a way to blend reading with using technology. For examples of book trailers, go to You-
Tube and search for "YALSA book trailers." There you will find book trailers for books
that were Morris Award and Nonfiction Award finalists, and book trailers for nominees for
YALSA's Teens' Top Ten, a booklist that is voted on by teens.

DISPLAYS AND BOOKLISTS

A way to do "stealth" readers' advisory is to create displays and booklists or bookmarks. These allow you to offer choices when you don't have time to do a one-on-one
readers' advisory interview.

Displays

Displays are limited only by your space and your imagination. Search Pinterest
(www.pinterest.com) for "teen book displays" to see many options. Book displays can
be grouped in any way that appeals to you: yellow books, books with shoes on the cover,
books that have been made into movies, road trip books, scary books, funny books, books
about heroes, or whatever strikes you. Book displays can be an excellent way to highlight
older books in your collection, especially when all your copies of the latest hot books are
checked out. You can just make a display that says, "Waiting for the new John Green book?
Try these now . . ."

Booklists

Similarly, booklists and bookmarks can be very handy to have around and a good
way to highlight items that may not be in the forefront of teens' minds. With software as
simple as Microsoft Word or Publisher or more complex graphic design software, you can
create attractive flyers or bookmarks with ease. Keep them simple, with relatively few titles
(10 to 15 is a good number) and leave them around the teen area.

CONCLUSION

Developing collections and doing readers' advisory for teens can be a challenge, but it can also be tremendously rewarding. Teens, unlike adults, are not yet completely set in their reading habits and are open to discovering new genres, new formats, new authors, and new styles. Yet, unlike children, they are able to read and understand complex narratives and even delight in immersing themselves in new and different worlds. As their ability to think abstractly grows, they can enjoy stories that jump back and forth in time, have multiple narrators, have unreliable narrators, or even include entirely made-up worlds, languages, and customs.

The key to providing teens with the kinds of books and other materials they want is to listen to them, engage in conversation with them, ask them questions, and be open to the answers. There is little in librarianship more gratifying than having a teenager come up to you and gush that the book you recommended is now his or her favorite book, or better yet, to have a teen tell you that he or she never read a book all the way through until you put that particular one in his or her hands. These affirmations make it worth doing the work that is required to know about YA literature and readers' advisory techniques.

REFERENCES

Aronson, Marc. 2001. *Exploding the Myths: The Truth about Teenagers and Reading*. Scarecrow Studies in Literature, No. 4. Lanham, MD: Scarecrow Press.

Burkey, Mary. 2012. *Audiobooks for Youth: A Practical Guide to Sound Literature*. Chicago: ALA Editions.

De la Peña, Matt. June 27, 2016. 2016 Newbery Acceptance Speech. *The Horn Book*. Available at: http://www.hbook.com/2016/06/news/awards/2016-newbery-acceptance-by-matt-de-la-pena/.

Goldsmith, Francisca. 2009. *The Readers Advisory Guide to Graphic Novels*. Chicago: ALA Editions.

Low, Jason T. June 17, 2013. "Why Hasn't the Number of Multicultural Books Increased in Eighteen Years?" Available at: http://blog.leeandlow.com/2013/06/17/why-hasnt-the-number-of-multicultural-books-increased-in-eighteen-years/.

Naidoo, Jamie Campbell. 2014. "The Importance of Diversity in Library Programs and Material Collections for Children." Association for Library Service to Children. Available at: http://www.ala.org/alsc/sites/ala.org.alsc/files/content /ALSCwhitepaper_importance%20of%20diversity_with%20graphics_FINAL.pdf.

CHAPTER 4

Programming for Teens

What does programming for teens mean? Programs are activities of interest to teens that the library provides or sponsors. Programs may be of educational value, or they may be purely entertainment. They may be one-time events, ongoing activities, or drop-in programs. But if they are not of interest or value to the teens themselves, they will be poorly attended. Vibrant teen programming depends on teen word-of-mouth, and the best way to get that is to get the teens involved in planning and creating your programs.

WHY DO PROGRAMS FOR TEENS?

We do programs for teens for the same reason we do programs for children or for adults: to provide recreational or educational opportunities for members of the community and to position the library as a place where people in the community can meet, learn, and grow. There might well be other reasons to provide programs—to market the library's materials and services, for example—but successful programs are going to arise out of a sincere desire to meet the needs of teens themselves.

Programs for teens give teens opportunities to:

- Create relationships with one another and with library staff
- Explore new ideas
- Express themselves creatively
- Use their time constructively

- Feel empowered
- Get support from nonparent adults
- Have fun!

Most of these go right back to the developmental assets and the concept of connected learning that were discussed in Chapter 1. Successful teen programs will meet the needs of the teens in your community and give them opportunities to explore, create, participate, and learn.

WHAT DO TEENS WANT IN A PROGRAM?

Of course, the real answer to this question is that you won't know until you ask them. The teens in your community are not generic teens. They have their own specific needs, interests, and desires, and the way to find out what kind of programming would appeal to them is to ask them. You can't just pull a program out of a box and expect that they will flock to it and love it. Start by finding out what they are interested in and what kinds of programs would draw them into the library. But here are some general ideas about the kinds of things that teens tend to look for in their programs.

- A chance to express their opinions and show their expertise. As we discussed in the first two chapters, teens are at the stage of their brain development where they are able to consider abstract concepts, and where they are beginning to figure out who they are and what their real interests are. They love to be asked for their opinions and to have opportunities to share what they know. Some types of programs that can fit into this need are:
  - *Book clubs.* These can be done in many different ways. Genre book clubs often work well—graphic novel book club, or fantasy book club, for example. Everyone can read the same book, or you can let each teen share with others what their current favorites are.
  - *Battle of the bands.* Let the teens show off their musical skills.
  - *Technology programs.* Gaming, of course, is always a favorite. "Technology Petting Zoos" allow teens to try out new gadgets, or, even better, to demonstrate them to adults. Or have the teens assist seniors in downloading music or audiobooks to tablets or smartphones.
  - *Art/photography shows.* You can display the teens' art or photos in the building, somewhere in the community, or on the library website. Invite art professors from a nearby college or professional artists and photographers to judge the entries.
  - *Writing contests.* Recruit teachers or writers to judge the entries, and post the winners on the website.
  - *Passive programs.* Later in this chapter, we'll talk more about passive programs, especially ones that allow for teen input and expertise.
- Time to hang out with friends. The library is one of the places in the community where teens can just enjoy being with their friends in a nonthreatening (and free) environment. Some types of programs that give them that opportunity are:
  - *Crafts.* Mine your library's staff for experts in various types of crafts, or look at some of the resources later in this chapter for suggestions.

- *Gaming*. Computer games, console games, and board games are all popular. If you have a space where they can play games and be with one another, this is a perennial favorite.
- *Drop-in programs*. If you have a dedicated space, you can set up a craft or project that teens can come in and try any time within a certain window: Saturday afternoons from 1 to 4, or after school on Thursdays from 4 until closing, for example. Or take part in the new craze of adult coloring books by having a large coloring sheet covering a table. Supply colored pencils or markers, and you're set.
- A safe place to try something new. As teens are finding themselves, library programs can give them the opportunity to try a new skill in a place of relative safety. Some examples are:
  - *Crafts*. Try a program to teach knitting, crochet, photography, cooking, scrapbooking, cake decorating, or whatever you have the space, expertise, and equipment for.
  - *Games*. Video games are always popular, but so are board games. Set up stations for chess, Settlers of Catan, Ticket to Ride, Sheriff of Nottingham, Pandemic, and more. See Board Game Geek (https://boardgamegeek.com/) for suggestions and reviews.
  - *Technology*. Not every teen is an expert at smartphone apps. Make an opportunity for them to share knowledge with one another and have an adult expert on hand to help.
  - *Physical activities*. Teaching various types of dance, martial arts, yoga, or whatever you have the space and expertise for.
  - *Life skills*. This could be anything from cooking and car repair to budgeting and test-taking.
- A way to make their mark. Teens want to matter. They want to help. The library can provide opportunities for them to be active members of the community:
  - *Volunteering*. Many libraries have teen volunteers who either do it for the fun and experience or to get community service hours for school. Keep a list of volunteer tasks handy.
  - *Community engagement*. If you are fortunate enough to live in a community that values teen involvement, partner with other organizations to come up with activities that your teens can do in the larger community, whether it's "clean-up days," helping out at the senior center or an afterschool program, or being part of a community event or festival.
  - *Helping younger kids*. Involve teens in helping out with Summer Reading, or in putting on programs for kids.
  - *Youth advisory*. A youth advisory board can help the library, by letting you know what the teens want and need. It can also help youth learn how to operate in a more formal setting, holding meetings, following agendas, and planning programs and activities.
- Something new and different. Teens, like everyone else, like to be involved in programs and activities that are out of their ordinary frame of reference. These tend to be bigger projects, and a small and understaffed (and underfunded) library may not be able to put in the resources required for these types of programs. Some examples are:
  - *Author visits*. Local authors are usually generous with their time for libraries. If you can't afford or don't have access to authors in person, many young adult (YA) authors are doing library visits via Skype. It never hurts to ask!

○ *Lock-ins*. Spending the night at the library may sound like a nightmare to you, but teens love it. It's an opportunity to hang out with friends, play some games, eat, watch some movies, and just generally have fun. Have lots of adult supervision!
○ *Readers' theater*. Check your collection or search online for readers' theater scripts. Give the teens a few minutes to read over the scripts and then they can perform them for one another or for a group of younger children.

PLANNING PROGRAMS

Although the tendency is to start with ideas for programs, it's actually best to start with evaluation. If you think first about how you will know if the program is a success, you stand a greater chance of making it one. So think about these questions:

- Who does the program serve? Are you doing this program because teens have been clamoring for it, or are you responding to a need expressed by teachers, parents, or library administrators?
- What do you hope that your audience will get out of the program? Will it address any of the aforementioned developmental assets (empowerment, engagement, creative expression)? Here are some possible things you might hope teens get out of a program:
  ○ To have fun in the library
  ○ To learn a skill
  ○ To be introduced to new technologies or materials
  ○ To meet like-minded teens
  ○ To have an opportunity to share their skills with others
  ○ To learn that the library and community value their interests
- What do you (the library) want to get out of the program? Maybe you are hoping to:
  ○ Raise library visibility
  ○ Increase circulation
  ○ Recruit teens for an advisory board
  ○ Have a positive public-relation event
  ○ Build community partnerships
  ○ Market library materials, services, and programs
- What impacts will the program or service have on the community at large? Will it engage teens and get them off the streets in those dangerous after-school hours? Will it affect the drop-out rate? Will it help them get jobs? Will it teach them a new skill? The answers to these questions may help you "sell" the program to your administration or other community partners.
- How will you know you have succeeded? Are you going to check circulation on certain items or certain types of items before and after? Are you going to do follow-up surveys?
- Who will you market it to? Will you market directly to teens or is your publicity more general—flyers in the library or notices on the website? Will you market to parents via the library's website or to teachers directly through the schools?
- How will you market it? Will you use the "spray and pray" method of spreading lots of flyers around and hoping someone will notice, or will you target specific groups or individuals? Will you do any one-on-one promotion? Will you go to schools? Will you send out e-mail or text blasts?

Planning Considerations

You have many aspects to consider when you start planning a program. All of them have some sort of cost, whether in time, staff resources, or just plain cash. Be sure to consider all of them so that you do not come up short at the last minute. Think about:

- *Space*. Where will you have your program? Does the library or some other community building have dedicated program space? How far in advance do you have to sign up for that space? Is the space appropriate to what you want to do? For example, you may want to do a painting program, but you can't because the space is carpeted and paint is not allowed.
- *Supplies*. What kinds of supplies will you need and how will you get them to the space? Will you need to buy supplies or does the library have a stock of supplies? How will you pay for the supplies? Does the library have an account with a local store, or do you buy things and get reimbursed, or do you have to order well ahead of time through library vendors?
- *Refreshments*. Food and drink are important to teenagers! Is there money to pay for food, or will you get it donated from local merchants? Can you have food and drink in the program space, or will you have to move to another area for refreshments? How much will you need?
- *Promotional costs*. This includes costs for flyers or other promotional items, your time to create the publicity and to distribute it. Will you be going to local schools to promote the program? Include your time as a cost, as well as mileage.
- *Staff*. This includes the time you spend planning and organizing the program, as well as the time you spend providing the program, cleaning up afterward, and evaluating it. And there will be other staff costs—someone to cover your desk hours during any part of the program planning and execution, for example, or extra clerks to handle increased circulation or manage crowds.
- *Equipment*. Think through what kinds of equipment you might need: audiovisual equipment, specialized equipment for the program, microphones, and so forth.
- *Budget*. How much is all of this going to cost? In the next section, we'll take a look at ways to pay for your programs.
- *Evaluation*. If you have started by thinking of evaluation, you will already know what it is that you want to know. So consider how you are going to find out. Will you do paper evaluations? Record comments? Count attendees?

Paying for Programs

Running programs costs money, one way or another. During your planning process, you should know exactly what your library will pay for (and how) and what you will have to find on your own. Here are some of the major ways that libraries pay for programs:

- *Budget line item*. If you are fortunate, your library has a budget line item for programs. It should be noted here that sometimes libraries plan for children's programs and even adult programs, but don't include teen programs. Find out. But even if the library does have a budget line for programs, there may be limitations on what can be purchased with the money, and on how it must be done. Know what you can and can't do before you get started.
- *Friends*. Many public libraries rely on Friends of the Library groups to support programming. As with the budget line item, there may be limitations and expectations. For

example, you may have to come up with a yearly budget to present ahead of time to the Friends Board for approval. Or they may pay for speakers or performers but not for food or supplies.

- *Grants.* Grants are available to libraries for programming. The Young Adult Library Services Association (YALSA) offers nearly $200,000 a year in grants to members, and some of that is for specific types of programs. They also sometimes partner with other organizations that provide grants for things like summer reading programs. It is well worth checking the website to find out if you are eligible (http://www.ala.org/yalsa/awardsandgrants/yalsaawardsgrants#awards). Sometimes stores like Target and Walmart offer grants to local schools and libraries.
- *Donations.* Often, local merchants will provide donations for library events. Find out from your director what the parameters are before you start asking, though—you don't want to ask Safeway to donate food for a teen program if the library has been planning to ask them to make a major donation for a larger event.

PUBLICITY AND MARKETING

No question that publicity and marketing for teen programs can be a challenge. The only really effective way to market is by word of mouth from other teens. Teenagers want to be where their friends are, and if another teen whom they know and like recommends a program, they will come. (Maybe. Assuming they have transportation. And assuming they don't have another commitment. And assuming they don't forget the time and place.)

So what is the librarian to do?

- Know your audience. Have a firm idea in your mind who it is that you are marketing to. Would it be more effective for your particular program to market it to parents or teachers? Is there a high school club that would be particularly interested in your program?
- Be authentic and don't try too hard. Don't spend hours on creating a cutesy flyer especially if you're not even sure your target audience will see it.
- Use "word of mouth." This can be especially effective if you have a teen advisory group that has been working with you to plan the program—they will make sure that their friends come. But think of other ways you can spread the word: the library's teenage pages and shelvers, the regulars who hang out in the library, the teenage children of the library's employees, and so on.
- Talk it up. Talk to the teens in your library. Tell them about the program. Talk to them some more. Tell them again. If you get even a nibble of interest, ask them to share the information with their friends.
- Use your library website, but bear in mind that many teens don't think of the website as a place to find information about programs of interest to them. If you have a teen Facebook page or Twitter account that actual teens use, then use that. But, again, those types of marketing are more likely to hit parents than teens.
- Use paper flyers as a last resort. Most people don't read signs, and teens are no exception. The best use of flyers is if you can get into a school and send them home with students. At least parents and teachers may see the flyers!

EVALUATION

As noted before, evaluation should begin during the planning process, as you determine what it is that you want to find out. But once you are underway, there are some ways to collect the information you need to help you plan your next program.

- *Pre- and post-program surveys*. If the purpose of your program is to teach a skill, you may want to know whether you did, in fact, teach that skill. In that case, you may want to do a quick pre-program survey of participants, in which you ask one or two questions about their current level of proficiency in that area. Then you can follow up with a post-program survey to find out if the level has improved.
- *User satisfaction survey*. Maybe the purpose of your program is just that the attendees have fun, hang out with others, enjoy the library, or even participate in providing some type of service. For those programs, you may want to follow up with a user satisfaction survey, asking if the program met their needs and/or expectations.
- *Staff survey or observation*. For some types of programs, especially drop-in programs, large events, or even passive programs, the easiest type of evaluation may be to collect information from other staff members. Ask them to record their observations of what went on: Did the teens appear to be enjoying themselves? Did the staff overhear conversations or observe interactions that related to the program and its goals?
- *Attendee comments*. If you have staff or volunteers to help, you can record attendee comments. You can ask them to write down comments, of course, but it's more effective to record them on a digital recorder or even a smartphone camera.
- *Attendance count*. Attendance can be important, especially to library administrators, but it is not the be-all and end-all. If you do capture attendance, make note of changes over time—is attendance growing or dropping at your teen programs? Which types of programs typically have larger attendance? Are there times of day or days of the week that draw larger crowds? Some programs, like craft programs, game programs, or various kinds of drop-in activities, may have an ebb and flow of attendance. It can be worthwhile to capture attendance numbers at 15-minute intervals in those cases.

PASSIVE PROGRAMS

Passive programs are the overworked librarian's best friend. Passive programs are simply activities that are not tied to a specific time or place. They are available for any teen who happens to be in the library (or even online, in some cases). Many passive programs work especially well if you have some wall space to post responses. Anything will do: a window, a blank wall, the endcaps of shelving units, or even a portable white board or bulletin board. Some advantages of passive programs are that they are:

- Less staff-intensive
- Great for the shy teen
- A way to meet kids one-on-one
- Great for occupying bored or rowdy kids

Examples of Passive Programs

- *Scavenger hunts.* Scavenger hunts can be done in many different ways. Look on Pinterest or just search on the web for "library scavenger hunts" to find examples. They can be educationally focused ("Where in the library would you find books on dinosaurs?") or just for fun (Find a book with _____ in the title. [a boy's name, an animal, a color, a number, etc.]). You can have the scavenger hunt sheets in your desk to hand out to kids who need something to do, or have them on a display, with the instruction that they are to turn them in to the desk when they are done. If they turn in a completed form, they can be entered into a drawing for a prize.
- *Twitter-style book reviews.* Ask teens to write a book review of a book (or movie or whatever) they liked in 140 characters or less. Post the results.
- *Guess the book from the tweet.* Start with a few of your own ("Looking forward to visiting the Burrow for winter break #gryffindorsrule" [Harry Potter]) and invite the teens to write and post their own.
- *Book faces.* Invite the teens to create photos of themselves holding book covers in place of their faces or other body parts. They find a book cover that has a picture of a face (or partial face, arm, leg, etc.). Then they pose with the book covering the corresponding part of their body. Post the results. Look up "book faces" online for examples.
- *First lines.* Post the first lines of famous books on a board. Have index cards or some other way for teens to write down what they think the book is, based on the first line.
- *Blackout poetry.* Take pages out of library discards and supply markers. The teens then black out parts of the page and highlight words to make a poem. Look up "blackout poetry" to find examples online.
- *Magnetic poetry.* Buy a box or two or three of magnetic poetry. Provide a space—the endcaps of metal library shelves work great, but you can also use a portable white board, or even metal cookie sheets or small white boards.
- *Book spine poetry.* See the web for many, many examples. Have your teens photograph their poems and post the photos.
- *Cover remix.* Provide paper and markers or colored pencils and ask the teens to draw their own versions of covers for their favorite books. Post results.
- *Cast the movie.* Pick a popular YA book that has not yet been made into a movie. Post a sheet with a list of characters and let them suggest which actors they would like to see in each part.
- *Shelftalkers.* Provide 3×5-inch cards for the teens to write short blurbs of books they like. Pull those books from the shelf and leave them on a book cart, with the cards taped to the cart.
- *Book soundtracks.* Ask teens to create a playlist or soundtrack for a favorite book. Post the results.

MAKING

Makerspaces are the latest rage in libraries (and elsewhere), but in fact library programs have long been about "making" of one kind or another. Do-it-yourself (DIY) projects and craft projects are staples of library programming. But are they the same thing as making? Well, it depends on your definitions. But, according to YALSA's *Making in the Library Toolkit* (YALSA 2014, 2), "Making, DIY and crafting are all hands-on, but the focus of making is to learn and ultimately innovate through doing and to leverage technologies to achieve that . . . Making focuses more on providing a social environment where students can develop new knowledge and skills that often can contribute to academic achievement or career preparation." Clearly, this definition of making falls directly into the same camp as connected learning—taking teen interests and helping them direct those toward larger personal achievement goals.

Making is not just about using technology, but rather about exploring and playing with technology and other kinds of things and actually to create something entirely new. As the YALSA toolkit (2014, 4) points out, "Libraries can provide access not only to information, but also the hands-on use and experience necessary to be a citizen in a digital world. By providing time and space allowing teens to experiment with tools they might not have anywhere else, we are bridging the digital divide, as well as helping teens build the skills they need to be successful in life and careers."

Of course, not every library has the space or the money to have a dedicated Makerspace, full of all kinds of tools, supplies, and equipment. But every library can encourage creative thinking and experimentation. Even occasional programs on topics like robotics, graphic design, computer programming, filmmaking, and so on are great kick-starters to get your teens thinking about making their own creations. Investing in some hardware and software, like Scratch (a program that teaches coding), Adobe Photoshop (to teach graphic design), Raspberry Pi (a low-cost, credit-card sized computer that plugs into a monitor or TV), Arduino (microcontroller-based kits for building digital devices), Sketchup (3D modeling software, similar to CAD), and GarageBand or LMMS (music production and mixing software) can be a cost- and space-effective way to get started with some making at your library. For suggestions on maker programs, check out the YALSA toolkit mentioned earlier (http://www.ala.org/yalsa/sites/ala.org.yalsa/files/content/MakingintheLibraryToolkit2014.pdf) or simply look up "STEM" or "Makerspace projects" on Pinterest (www.pinterest.com).

ADULT SKILLS AND WORKFORCE DEVELOPMENT

Keep in mind that not all programming for teens has to be aimed at recreational activities. Teens in many communities are dealing with the realities of approaching adulthood and how to prepare themselves for the future. The programs below can be a good opportunity for you to form partnerships with members of your local community, including educators, bank employees or financial planners, nutritionists, members of the trades, and others who can be resources for the programs described. Remember, you don't have to do everything yourself. Depending on your community, you may find a strong audience for programs such as:

- *SAT, ACT, ASVAB, or GED preparation.* Obviously, these are different audiences, but many teens are going to be faced with some kind of standardized testing. Many libraries have online test prep software (such as Learning Express), but a course on tips and tricks for taking standardized tests can be very popular.
- *Workforce development workshops.* Teens are finding it harder and harder to get jobs. According to a report by Career Builder (2015, 14), 33 percent fewer teens (aged 14–18) held jobs in 2014 than in 2001. Teens lost a significant share in the types of jobs that used to be staples of after-school and summer employment: dishwashers, fast-food

workers, ushers and ticket-takers at movie theaters. Without those types of experiences, teens nearing high school graduation need help in basics such as:

- How to interview for a job
- Filling out online applications
- Writing a resume
- Basic information about entry-level jobs

- *Job readiness.* In addition to just getting a job, teens may be completely uninformed about what is necessary to hold and keep a job. Invite a selection of local supervisors and managers (including those from your own library) to host a panel discussion on the kinds of things supervisors expect from entry-level workers, from showing up on time to appropriate apparel.

- *Life skills.* Whether the teens in your community are headed for college or the work-force, they may find that a program or workshop on one or more of these basic life skills would be useful:

  - *Budgets and money.* The realities of credit-card debt, how to get (and pay off) a loan, online banking, and how to make and keep a budget.
  - *Food skills.* Reading labels, reading recipes, maintaining a balanced diet, using basic kitchen equipment. For those about to go to college, try a "Dorm Room Cooking" class.
  - *Clothing-related skills.* How to do laundry, how to mend clothes and sew on buttons, how to pack a suitcase, how to shop for clothes that will be a good value.
  - *Car skills.* How to check oil and washer fluid and add more, how to check tire pressure and add air, how to change a tire, how to jump-start a car, how to buy a car.
  - *Home skills.* From fixing toilets, changing fuses, and cleaning out the lint trap on the dryer to basic housecleaning tips: how to clean wood floors, or grout, or the tile in your shower.
  - *Etiquette.* Writing thank-you notes, table manners, gift-giving, telephone manners, and more.

College Readiness

In addition to test preparation programs, as mentioned earlier in the text, there are other ways libraries can help teens prepare for the major life change of attending college. In an article in *Young Adult Library Services* (*YALS*), Amanda Ochsner (2016, 16) notes that "research suggests that a critical reason why many students do not attend college is not that they are not qualified but because they lack the knowledge and skills to navigate the process of applying to college and for financial aid." This is certainly true of students who come from families where college is not a given. Ochsner describes several games that have been developed by the Pullias Center for Higher Education at the University of Southern California (USC) that can be used by libraries to help teens navigate the application process. Using proven platforms, from card games to iPad apps to online content, the games help teens learn something about colleges themselves as well as the admission process. For more details, see Ochsner's article or http://www.gameinnovationlab.com.

Citizenship

Teens who are finishing high school are old enough or almost old enough to vote. In many communities, libraries serve as polling places on Election Day, which provides a ready-made opportunity to engage teens in the political life of their community, state, and nation. Team up with the League of Women Voters (http://lwv.org) or Project Vote Smart (http://votesmart.org) to present programs on the issues in the upcoming election.

In 2001, the American Library Association (ALA) created a document called *Smart Voting Starts @ Your Library*. It contains many ideas that libraries can use in educating their communities about voting, including a number that can be adapted for use with teens. For example:

- Host an event in which teens watch a political debate and discuss the issues afterward.
- Sponsor a forum on local issues, inviting candidates for local offices to answer questions from local teens.
- Have a movie night, showing a film about American politics. Optionally, invite a local professor or teacher to moderate a discussion afterward. Movies could include titles like *Mr. Smith Goes to Washington, Advise and Consent, All the King's Men, Seven Days in May, All the President's Men, The Candidate, The Manchurian Candidate, Election, Lincoln*, or *Wag the Dog*. Be sure you have public performance rights for the movie!
- Work with teachers at the local high school and sponsor a debate at the library in which students represent the positions of candidates—this could be presidential candidates or candidates for state or local offices.

TIPS AND TRICKS

Don't be afraid of programming for teens. If you try something and it doesn't work, try something else. Meanwhile, here are some basic things to keep in mind:

- Get the teens involved in planning and implementing your programs.
  - Ask for their input upfront.
  - Create opportunities for them to share their opinions and their expertise.
  - Give them options.
  - Display their work.
- Keep in touch with area schools—they can help you spread the word, and even give you ideas for appropriate programs.
- Locate coworkers who might be helpful—by offering their skills as presenters or teachers, or just as enthusiastic kid-wranglers.
- If you run into obstacles, step back and reevaluate.
- Don't forget about passive programming.
- Have food!

BOOKS AND WEBSITES FOR TEEN PROGRAMS

Books

Alessio, Amy, ed. 2008. *Excellence in Library Services to Young Adults*, 5th edition. Chicago: YALSA.

Alessio, Amy and Kimberly Patton. 2011. *A Year of Programs for Teens 2*. Chicago: ALA Editions.

Alexander, Linda B. and Nahyun Kwon, eds. 2010. *Multicultural Programming for Tweens and Teens*. Chicago: ALA Editions.

Coleman, Tina and Peggie Llanes. 2013. *The Hipster Librarian Guide to Teen Craft Projects 2*. Chicago: ALA Editions.

Fink, Megan, ed. 2011. *Teen Read Week and Teen Tech Week: Tips and Resources for YALSA's Initiatives*. Chicago: YALSA.

Helmrich, Erin and Elizabeth Schneider. 2011. *Create, Relate, and Pop @ the Library: Services and Programs for Teens & Tweens*. New York: Neal-Schuman.

Lillian, Jenine, ed. 2009. *Cool Teen Programs for Under $100*. Chicago: YALSA.

Ott, Valerie. 2006. *Teen Programs with Punch: A Month-by-Month Guide*. Westport, CT: Libraries Unlimited.

Starkey, Monique Delatte, ed. 2013. *Practical Programming: The Best of YA-YAAC*. Chicago: YALSA.

YALSA. 2012. *The Complete Summer Reading Manual: From Planning to Evaluation*. Chicago: YALSA.

Websites

Ohio Library Council: http://olc.org/pdf/YA_TeenProgramGuide122010.pdfolc.org/pdf/YA_TeenProgramGuide122010.pdf
Activities and program ideas for every month.

Pinterest site by Andrea Graham: www.pinterest.com/4ya
Links to all kinds of teen crafts and programs.

Teen Librarian Toolbox: teenlibrariantoolbox.com
Resources for teen librarians, including "Teen Programs in a Box"—prepackaged (but adaptable) programs for use in libraries.

Teen Services Underground: www.teenservicesunderground.com/programming/a-z-program-list/
An A-Z list of programs described in detail by actual YA librarians.

Teen Tech Week: teentechweek.ning.com
Resources for YALSA's annual Teen Tech Week.

YALSA College and Career Readiness Wiki: http://wikis.ala.org/yalsa/index.php/College_%26_Career_Readiness

YALSA Maker Toolkit: www.ala.org/yalsa/sites/ala.org.yalsa/files/content/MakingintheLibraryToolkit2014.pdf
Toolkit for maker programs in the library.

YALSA Programming Wiki: wikis.ala.org/yalsa/index.php/Main_Page#Programming_
Resources
Basic information on programming resources.

YALSA Teen Programming Guidelines: http://www.ala.org/yalsa/teen-programming-
guidelines
Guidelines for teen programming in the library.

REFERENCES

ALA. 2001. "Smart Voting Starts @ Your Library." Available at: http://www.ala.org/
aboutala/sites/ala.org.aboutala/files/content/governance/officers/kranich_2.pdf.

Career Builder. March 2015. "The Changing Face of US Jobs." Available at: http://career
buildercommunications.com/pdf/changing-face-of-us-jobs.pdf.

Ochsner, Amanda. Summer 2016. "College Access." *Young Adult Library Services (YALS)*
14(4): 16–17.

YALSA. 2014. "Making in the Library Toolkit." Available at: http://www.ala.org/yalsa/
sites/ala.org.yalsa/files/content/MakingintheLibraryToolkit2014.pdf.

YALSA. 2016. "College and Career Readiness Wiki." Available at: http://wikis.ala.org/
yalsa/index.php/College_%26_Career_Readiness.

CHAPTER 5

Teens and Their Information Needs

A common interaction that library staff members have with teens is the reference transaction. For the most part, working with teens is no different from working with any other library user. Good customer service skills are the key. Just like adults, teens want answers—correct answers—to the questions they ask. They also want to be treated with respect, they want to feel good about the interaction, and they often want to learn something so they can be more independent in the future. While an adult may feel comfortable about "interrupting" a staff member who appears to be busy, teens often lack the self-confidence to approach such a person. That's why it is critical for librarians and other library staff to appear inviting and approachable. Teens may feel that they appear to be stupid when asking for help, so it is the staff persons' job to make it clear that there is nothing they want more than to help them answer their questions. Approaching teens with a question like "Are you finding everything you need?" or "Hi, how can I help?" gives them the opportunity to ask for help without losing face. Also remember that teens are less able than adults to interpret facial expressions accurately. What you think is a neutral expression can appear to a teen to be a "mean" look.

INFORMATION-SEEKING BEHAVIOR

Like many adult library users, teens often begin by asking the question they think you can answer, rather than the question they really have. This goes for both the questions they ask library staff and the queries they enter into the library catalog or web search engine.

For example, they will ask if the library has "any books about war" when their assignment is to write an essay on the causes of World War I. Or they will enter the search term "World War I" into Google and either become alarmed at the vast amount of information that shows up or simply take the first hit—which is probably a Wikipedia article—and fail to go any further.

Many library staff members assume that information is best acquired through what are known as "formal" information systems: catalogs, directories, books, formally organized websites, and so on. Teens (and many adults), on the other hand, tend to prefer "informal" information systems, in which they don't so much search for information as share it. This tendency has been reinforced by the use of the Internet and social networking. Teens often view social sharing sites as the best places to answer their personal or popular culture queries. Also, teens have grown up doing "group work" in school, and many of them prefer to do their library work that way, as well. They will have their friends around them at the computer as they search for information, and they will use feedback from friends to help them find the answers.

Imposed versus Personal Queries

Teens tend to approach library staff with two main kinds of questions. The most common is the "imposed query," a question imposed on them by a teacher or other adult, usually a homework assignment. In many cases, the teens themselves are not particularly interested in the answer; they just know they have to have it (immediately!). The other main kind of question is the "personal query," which can range from popular culture interests to career or college information to recreational reading.

Both of these kinds of queries can and do cause problems for library workers. Staff may dislike imposed queries because teens don't really seem that invested in the answer or don't even know what the real question is. There can be a sense that helping with these queries is somehow unfair and that library staff shouldn't be "doing their homework for them." Personal queries can seem to library staff to be problematic in a different way. If they involve popular culture topics, library staff may not even have heard of the topic yet. A fear of looking foolish or a sense that all such topics are ephemeral and unimportant can cause staff to dismiss these queries without making much effort. To complicate matters, many of the formal information sources that librarians are accustomed to using may not have much information on these topics. Some personal queries may deal with issues that teens are reluctant to discuss out loud, such as sexuality or drugs. Still others may be easier for library staff to deal with, like career or college information, or information about hobbies or sports.

In all cases, good customer service dictates that we give teens and their questions respect and take them seriously. Library staff should always regard the teens' questions as important.

If you are unfamiliar with the topic, you can make the teen's question an opportunity to learn something, or even possibly to improve your library's service to the community by adding a resource. Taking this opportunity to provide a positive library experience for teens is a great way to help teens grow, and at the same time, it creates a healthier and better integrated community. If teens see the library as a place that takes them seriously and has something to offer them, they will be more likely to become and remain library supporters in the future.

DEALING EFFECTIVELY WITH SCHOOL ASSIGNMENTS

Homework is a major reason for teens to engage in information-seeking. But public libraries have a very different approach to the homework issue than school libraries do. School libraries have collections that are focused on the curriculum. Where there is a school librarian, that person is usually also a teacher, and his or her main job is to teach the students how to use the library, find resources, evaluate sources, and meet the curriculum goals as determined by the teachers.

Public libraries, on the other hand, have a different charge. The collection, while it may contain materials that will help with homework queries, is usually much broader than a school library, while at the same time being less deep in specific areas. Reference staff at a public library is geared toward helping all users, no matter the age, find the best information. So the focus is more on the "what" than the "how"—finding the answer, rather than learning how to find the answer. This can, of course, cause frustration for the public librarian, especially when teens don't seem especially interested in doing any of the work themselves. Librarians may complain, "He just wants me to do his homework for him!"

You need to recognize the reality of homework needs and find ways to facilitate it. It can be useful to start by understanding the particularities of your situation. For example, how many schools are in the library's service area? This will affect the number of assignments and the kinds and amounts of materials you will need to have in the collection. It is also useful to know how well-funded and well-equipped the schools are and whether or not they have good libraries with strong collections and professional librarians. If teens are getting training in information literacy at school and if their schools have the materials (including databases) that they need for most assignments, the public library's role will be different from that in a community where the school libraries have basically nothing.

Likewise, it is useful to know about the demographics of the community. Do most families have computers and reliable broadband access at home, or do they rely on the public library for access to the web? Is the school library available to students before and after school? And is the public library easily accessible to teens? Can they get there on their own, or do they need an adult to give them a ride. The answer to these questions will affect the times and days that teens are at the library.

Curriculum Needs

The next step is to know the curriculum needs. It is much easier to help a teen with a homework assignment if you know what the assignment actually is. There are several ways to do this. If you have a good relationship with the local schools, it is possible that you can find out directly from the school librarian or teachers. In the real world, however, getting that information can be a real challenge. However, you can start by approaching school library staff. This can be difficult in locations where there is no school librarian but only a volunteer. In those cases, you might consider contacting department heads (in middle schools and high schools) or grade team leaders (in elementary schools) to find out if there are any new topics or approaches in the coming year. You can also share information with them about new resources in the library.

Even without that contact, knowing the local curriculum isn't all that complicated. Your school district will have the basic information, such as what is taught in each year: American history in 5th, 8th, and 11th grades, for example, ancient civilizations in 6th grade and medieval and renaissance times in 7th grade. From experience in the library, library staff will know something about the common recurring assignments, such as state reports for fifth-graders and American literature projects for high school juniors.

Don't forget about private schools in your service area, too. They may have somewhat different curricula, but the same general rules apply.

Homework Alerts

Homework alerts are a way for teachers to let you know in advance about the kinds of projects and assignments that typically send kids to the public library for more information. You can create a printed version or put a form on your library's website (search online for "homework alert form" for lots of examples). These give teachers a quick and easy way to let the public library know about upcoming assignments and to give you information that will help you help their students: when the assignment is due, the types of materials that may or may not be used, and so on. It also gives you a chance to contact the teacher with information that may help him or her, such as which library databases would be most useful, or the fact that the library has a great new series on inventors, but that all of the books are 96 pages, so they might want to rethink the "100 or more pages" requirement.

However, homework alert forms are not necessarily the answer to all your problems. As Carol Intner (2011, 38) says in her book *Homework Help from the Library*:

> Don't be surprised if teachers are not as enthusiastic as you are about the idea of homework alerts. On the one hand, most teachers welcome support from the library for their instruction. On the other hand, they may feel that filling out the form for each major assignment is yet one more detail they need to take care of among the ever-growing administrivia on their plates. Any ideas to shorten the amount of time and effort required to fill out the form will win more cooperation from teachers.

Intner suggests check boxes instead of fill-in-the-blank for questions such as the type of material that may be used, for example.

Copies of Assignments

Many school districts provide an online calendar or other website that contains homework assignments, organized by teacher or subject matter. Some of these are accessible to the public; if one requires a log-in, ask a teen or parent to show you the site so you can see the assignment for yourself. In addition, school library websites sometimes include links to homework assignments. Consider asking your teen volunteers to monitor the homework sites on a regular basis and alert you to new and upcoming assignments that might bring students to the public library.

If you don't have information from the school, try to find a teen who has a written copy of the assignment, then make a photocopy and keep it at the reference desk. Not only will it help you narrow the search, but it will help the library staff who get the same question from the next five (or fifty) teens. Some libraries keep an assignment binder or a file on a reference desk computer that notes the best resources you have found for the various assignments. Also, be aware that there are frequently recurring topics for school assignments, such as science projects, literary criticism, author biographies, and U.S. history.

Pathfinders

Your library may have print or online pathfinders with selected resources for common homework assignments. Take advantage of these or create them if they don't exist. Also, use the expertise of other libraries: many library websites have a "homework help" section under their Teen Services page that lists good resources for common homework questions. It is worth taking a look at the websites of some of the larger libraries to see what kinds of things they link to in their homework help sections. Try Los Angeles Public Library (www.lapl.org/teens/homework-help), King County (WA) Library (www.kcls.org/teens/homework.cfm), or San Francisco Public Library (http://themixatsfpl.org/).

Textbooks

The decision to add textbooks to the collection will vary from library to library, depending on the collection development policy, budget constraints, and other administrative decisions. If you do collect textbooks, you will have to decide whether to make them circulating or reference. One advantage to having textbooks is that they can be a big help to library workers trying to identify the exact assignment. Another is simply that having textbooks is a service to students who are at the public library but have left their textbook(s) at home or school. On the other hand, it can be nearly impossible to be certain that the library has all of the necessary textbooks, in all the right editions, and unless they are a noncirculating collection, the one the student wants may not be there. Even if textbooks don't circulate, if you only have one of each, it may be in use by another student.

THE REFERENCE INTERVIEW

The reference interview with a teen follows the same techniques as any reference interview. Try to identify what the teen really wants to know. Ask questions like:

- What are you working on?
- What are you trying to understand?
- What would you like to know about x?
- What sort of thing are you looking for?
- What requirements do you have for this (project, assignment, etc.)?
- What have you done about this question so far? Where have you looked?
- What did your teacher tell you about this topic?
- What else can you tell me about what you're working on?
- What would help you the most?

Ask open questions (not yes/no questions) but be sure to use voice tones and expressions that turn the questions into a conversation, not a battery of inquiries that can make the teen feel quizzed.

Once the question is clarified, help teens by empowering them to work independently. Many teens are certain they already know all there is to know about the library, but it is almost always possible to astonish them by showing them how to use a database of which they weren't aware or a neat tip or trick about the library catalog. This allows you to be a guide—not an information gatekeeper—and it shows respect for the teen user. Always explain what you are doing and where you are going.

After finding some sources for the teen, be sure to ask if the need has been met or if follow-up is needed. Say things like:

- Does this completely answer your question?
- Is that the kind of material or information you were hoping to get?
- Will this help you?
- Are you finding what you're looking for?
- Is there anything else I can help you with?
- If this doesn't do the trick, please come back and we'll see what else we can find.

Sources

The best way to help teens with reference queries is to be aware of your library's resources. Know what is in your collection, and know what databases you have and how to use them effectively. Keep in mind that teens are hypercritical of adults, so if you can't use your own library's databases, or fumble around without helping, they will not be likely to trust your expertise in the future. In addition, be aware of online resources that might be useful for teens. Remember that most teens are transliterate, as we discussed in Chapter 3. They may find a podcast or a video to be the best way to learn about a new topic. It is a good idea to familiarize yourself with a few good sources for multimedia approaches to standard homework topics. Even if they can't use these in their bibliography, they might be a good place to start.

John and Hank Green's "Crash Course" YouTube channel (https://www.youtube .com/user/crashcourse) contains 10–15 minute videos on topics in U.S. and world history, literature, biology, ecology, and chemistry. The Khan Academy (www.khanacademy.org) has short videos on practically any topic a teenager might come across in school. In the iTunes Store you can find videos and podcasts, many of them free, on many different topics. The Library of Congress (www.loc.gov) has more and more content online, including films, maps, sound recordings, historic newspapers, photographs, and more. Most of the educational television channels like PBS, National Geographic, and The History Channel have extensive online archives. BBC Radio 4 produces weekly podcasts on historical, scientific, and cultural topics in their "In Our Time" program, and all episodes are free to download (http://www.bbc.co.uk/programmes/b006qykl). These are just a few examples of high-quality materials that are available online and that could be useful to teens working on projects or just interested in various topics. Use your own information-seeking skills to locate other, similar sites that will be of use to teens in doing their homework or expanding their own knowledge.

PERSONAL QUERIES

The same techniques, of course, apply to personal queries as to homework queries. In this case, however, the interview may be difficult for a variety of reasons. If the personal query is of a sensitive nature, it may take some effort to draw the teen out about what he or she really needs. Remember that teens are very self-conscious, and they constantly feel that others (especially adults) are judging them. They are more inclined to wander about and do their own searches if the topic is one of a personal or sensitive nature. This is also why books about drugs, alcohol, and sexuality often disappear from libraries: a teen would rather steal the book than let someone see that he or she is checking it out.

The best way to deal with these types of queries is to be as matter-of-fact as you would when searching for information about any other, more neutral, topic. You want to send the teen to the most reliable information you can find on whatever the topic is. This may be an opportunity to help a teen learn how to evaluate a website's reliability, currency, authority, and bias (or lack thereof). This is also a place where the library's databases may come in handy. Teens are often unaware of these useful resources.

If the personal query is not so much sensitive as it is esoteric, the first step may be to find out as much as you can about the topic from the teen. Use the query as an opportunity to learn about a topic that is new to you and consider where you might find materials on the subject, whether online or in databases.

INFORMATION LITERACY

Information literacy is the ability to recognize a need for information and then effectively identify, locate, evaluate, and use that information. In many states there are fewer and fewer school librarians, so teens learn the skills of information literacy, not in a special library class but rather in working with teachers and classmates on research projects or from staff at the public library who are helping them with assignments. These skills will help teens become independent users of libraries, and that in turn will help them be successful not only in school but also as lifelong learners.

Some of the critical information literacy skills that teens need to develop include an understanding of:

- How information is organized, both in the library and on the Internet
- Different types of searches, such as keyword and subject searches and ways to refine those searches
- How the library catalog works
- Which subscription databases the library has and how they can be helpful
- How to evaluate websites for accuracy, completeness, and objectivity
- How to cite sources
- Information ethics

Many of these skills can be modeled during everyday reference transactions with teens. For example, if a teen asks where to find a certain book, walk with the teen to the catalog and help with the search, noting the various ways to search (by keyword, title, author, etc.). If it seems appropriate, show some of the other features of the catalog, such as limiting by format or location, sorting by date, or clicking on a subject heading to find related materials. Or, for example, while walking to the stacks with a teen to find a book for a report, point out that the library is organized by subject and that there are likely to be other books on a similar topic nearby.

HOMESCHOOLERS

According to the National Center for Education Statistics (NCES 2012), about 3 percent of school-aged children in the United States are homeschooled. Many of these homeschoolers are avid library users. Meeting the information needs of homeschooling teens is not a lot different from meeting the needs of those in schools. One of the major differences may be that the homeschooled teen is more likely to be researching a topic of his or her own interest rather than be trying to answer an imposed query. Librarians can help homeschooled teens by teaching them about library databases and by working with them on evaluating websites. One advantage to working with the homeschooled teen is that you may be more likely to be able to work with them in the hours of the day when the library is less busy.

In her book *Helping Homeschoolers in the Library* (2009), Adrienne Furness lists 10 things libraries can do to provide better service to homeschoolers in the public library. Here are a few of those things:

- Talk to homeschoolers in your library and find out what they are working on and what kinds of help they want.
- Connect with homeschooling groups in the community and help them connect with one another.
- Allow and encourage homeschoolers to use library meeting room space.
- Display projects created by homeschoolers.
- Offer homeschoolers any privileges you offer teachers (extended loan periods, increased item limits, fine waivers, etc.).
- Attend local homeschooling events and conferences to make connections and find out what is going on.

USING THE WEB

Teens will almost always want to start any project by searching on the web. However, many do not have the skills to evaluate a site to determine whether the information provided there is accurate and authoritative. This is one of the most valuable skills library workers can teach teens. It can start with something as simple as pointing out the difference between ads and relevance-ranked results on common search engines like Google. But ultimately, teens should be shown how to evaluate a site's purpose, authority, accuracy, and bias. The University of California (Berkeley) Library has created a very useful page (http://www.lib.berkeley.edu/TeachingLib/Guides/Internet/Evaluate.html) on techniques to apply and questions to ask when evaluating a website. It takes the user through the process of determining what the URL itself can indicate, how to find information about the author of the site, and some of the things that indicate whether the information provided is of good quality. Teens want to be "in the know," so teaching them some of these helpful tricks can impress them and enable them to impress their friends.

Many teachers prohibit the use of Wikipedia in school assignments, but often Wikipedia is actually a good place to start. Teach teens a few simple tricks for using Wikipedia effectively. For example, point out the footnotes (clicking on a footnote number takes you to the notes section of the article) and the references. Any time you see a link, it will give you even more information. The references section of a Wikipedia article includes complete bibliographic information for works cited. If a book is mentioned, you can look it up to see if the library has it—and Wikipedia has actually made that easy by including an

OCLC number. Clicking on the OCLC number directs you to the WorldCat record for the book, which indicates which libraries hold it. Clicking on the ISBN takes the user to a page where you can sometimes find a link to a Google Books search for the book. In Google Books, you may be able to look at some or all of the books cited. Showing teens how to use the footnotes and references in Wikipedia can help them understand how Wikipedia articles are created, and it can point them toward specific print and online sources that they can use in their own bibliographies.

THE LIBRARY'S ONLINE PRESENCE

According to the 2013 report "Teens and Technology," by the Pew Research Center, in collaboration with the Berkman Center for Internet and Society at Harvard:

- Ninety-five percent of teens (aged 12–17) use the Internet.
- Ninety-three percent of teens have a computer or access to one at home.
- Twenty-three percent of teens have a tablet computer.
- Seventy-eight percent of teens have a cell phone, and almost half (47%) of those are smartphones, which means 37 percent of teens have smartphones, up from 23 percent in 2011.
- Seventy-four percent of teens say they access the Internet on mobile devices at least occasionally.
- Twenty-five percent say they access the Internet *mostly* on their cell phones. (Madden 2013a)

In another report from Pew and Berkman, "Teens, Social Media, and Privacy," from May 2013, researchers report that the typical (median) teen Facebook user has 300 friends, and the typical teen Twitter user has 79 followers. Sixty percent of teen Facebook users keep their profiles private (limited to friends) and have confidence in their ability to maintain their online privacy. Consequently, they share a great deal of personal information about themselves in these social media outlets (Madden 2013b).

These numbers are changing every year. In May 2015, Pew reported that 88 percent of U.S. teens had access to a smartphone or cell phone, and 9 percent of those teens exchange texts, an average of 30 texts per day (Lenhart 2015).

Clearly teens are online, and the library must be online, as well. Many libraries have a teen page as part of their website. This can be a good way to introduce teens to the many services that the library has to offer, from materials and reading suggestions to programs and opportunities to volunteer. Many libraries offer virtual reference service, either through instant messaging or through subscription services like Brainfuse and Tutor.com. Others have a library account on a social networking site, like Facebook, Twitter, or LibraryThing. These provide opportunities for the library to market programs and services directly to teens and for teens to interact through comments or postings.

Teens want to use the library when it is convenient for them—not only when it is convenient for the library to be open. The library may close at 9 p.m., but 9 p.m. to midnight may be the prime homework time for teens. Besides teaching teens how to use the library's online resources while they are in the library, provide online tutorials on the library's website to help them use the library when it is closed.

CONCLUSION

Helping teens with their information needs is often a librarian's best opportunity to create relationships. At some time or other, most teens will need to come to the library for homework help or other research and having a good reference transaction can build trust. When teens see that you have treated their questions and requests with respect, privacy, and competence, they will be more likely to come to you in the future with other requests, including those of a more personal nature. Building that trust is good for the library and good for the teenager, who will come to understand the role of the library in the community and in his or her own development.

REFERENCES

Furness, Adrienne. 2009. *Helping Homeschoolers in the Library*. Chicago: ALA Editions.

Intner, Carol. 2011. *Homework Help from the Library: In-Person and Online*. Chicago: ALA Editions.

Lenhart, Amanda. April 9, 2015. "Teens, Social Media, and Technology Overview 2015." Available at: http://www.pewinternet.org/2015/04/09/teens-social-media-technology-2015/.

Madden, Mary, et al. March 13, 2013a. "Teens and Technology 2013." Available at: http://www.pewinternet.org/2013/03/13/teens-and-technology-2013/.

Madden, Mary, et al. May 21, 2013b. "Teens, Social Media, and Privacy." Available at: http://www.pewinternet.org/2013/05/21/teens-social-media-and-privacy/.

NCES. 2012. "Fast Facts: Homeschooling." Available at: http://nces.ed.gov/FastFacts/display.asp?id=91.

CHAPTER 6

Teen Spaces

Not every library has enough space to have a fully equipped and dedicated teen room. But every library can create a space—and an entire library—that is teen-friendly. In this chapter, we'll talk about the creation of separate teen spaces and also about how to go about making your library friendly to teens through your policies, practices, and procedures.

TEEN-FRIENDLY LIBRARIES

In a position paper for the Young Adult Library Services Association (YALSA) on teen spaces and public libraries, Kimberly Bolan (2016) states, "Libraries are essential informal learning spaces within communities that bridge the gap between the classroom and afterschool, and they provide an ideal environment for all teens to engage in connected learning activities—hands-on, teen-driven activities that enable teens to learn while exploring their passions and interests." Bolan points out that creating a teen-oriented space in a public library is one way to create a positive and safe environment for teens and to acknowledge their unique needs. This, in turn, gives them a sense of belonging in the community, as well as a feeling of ownership of the space.

If you are building a new library in the 21st century, you will almost certainly want to include a dedicated space for teens, and you will have plenty of help to achieve that goal. Architects, library building planners, library administrators and others are all well aware of the current trends in young adult (YA) spaces. Nevertheless, it is essential to get teen engagement and participation in planning a new teen space.

In an article in *Public Libraries Online*, Meghann Kuhlmann et al. (2014) report on a grant project in which librarians and teens were interviewed about public library teen spaces. They note:

> In all YA space design decisions, local teen voices should receive the highest possible respect and value . . . librarians must actively solicit teen input and provide environments supportive of meaningful evaluation activities. Above all, it is essential to remember that YA library spaces are intended to benefit teens in the ways they choose to interact with and within them.

They also noted that teens and librarians had different interests and concerns when thinking about library spaces. Librarians were more concerned with materials and resources, while teens wanted to talk about what they actually did while in the library: activities and experiences rather than resources and materials.

Of course, most librarians will never have the opportunity to create a space from the ground up and will have to find a way to make an attractive and useful teen space within their current walls. It can be done! Start, as with all teen programs and services, by finding out what the local teens need and want. And don't just ask the teens who are already library users: designing a new teen space—or renovating an old one—is an excellent opportunity to bring in voices from teens who currently do not use the library but would if they could find what they need there. So the more teen input you can get into the planning process, the better.

Make YALSA's National Teen Space Guidelines (http://www.ala.org/yalsa/guidelines/teenspaces) your bible for designing and implementing a teen space in your library. These guidelines address both physical and virtual teen spaces in public libraries and apply even to libraries in which the teen space is not separate from the rest of the library. The guidelines suggest, among many other things, that the library environment should:

- Be comfortable, inviting, open, and have a vibrant and teen-friendly look and feel.
- Accommodate individual as well as group use for socializing and learning.
- Allow for ample display of teen print, artistic, and digital creations.
- Contribute to a sense of teen belonging, community involvement, and library appreciation.

TEEN OWNERSHIP OF THE SPACE

If at all possible, a teen space should be just that—for teens. Not every library can accomplish this feat, of course. But if you do have a separate space for teens, make it a library policy to limit adult use of that space, at least during the most popular after-school and evening hours. This allows teens to feel comfortable and safe in their own space. If adults are hanging around all the time, teens will gravitate away from the space. Teens may seem confident and self-assured, but they will find it difficult to ask an adult to vacate their space.

POLICIES

Library policies can be made teen-friendly as well. This does not mean that teens should be allowed to run wild over the library. But it does mean that teens should be treated with respect for their age and abilities in your library's policies and in the enforcement of those policies. Here are some examples:

- *Noise policies.* Enforce noise policies fairly. Many libraries seem to think that noisy toddlers and story time caregivers are just fine, but noisy teens are a problem.
- *Furniture policies.* Is it really necessary to have, for example, a policy that allows "only 4 to a table"? What is the problem the policy is trying to solve? Is there another way it can be solved?
- *Circulation policies.* Are there different borrowing periods or fines for teen materials? Is a driver's license or other formal identification card required to obtain a library card? Often minors, even teenagers, don't have this type of state-issued identification. Ideally, there should be other options, such as using a school ID or mailing a postcard to the home address, and bringing it back to prove the address. And it is a barrier to teen access to require a parent's signature on a library card. Is this really necessary? Is parental permission required for minors to have access to certain parts of the collection? These are all issues that may need to be taken up with the library director, board of trustees, or city government. But it is worth examining the library's policies to see which ones make it more difficult for teens to use the library and then seeing if it is possible to change them.
- *Computer and Internet access policies.* Do teens have the same time limits as everyone else? Are teens limited to filtered computers? Again, find out the basis of this policy and determine whether it can be changed to make teen access more equitable to that of adults. Bear in mind that teen homework needs require full access to the Internet these days.
- *Volunteer policies.* Today many teens are required to do service hours in order to graduate from high school, so it is likely that you will see teens showing up to look for opportunities to volunteer at the library. Your library's volunteer policies should be clear about your expectations and about the kind of work volunteers can do. There is no reason why teens cannot do most or all of the same kinds of volunteer tasks that adults do. They will want to do something that feels meaningful, and most will want to do something that is more active than just sitting at a table cutting out shapes for story time. If you can involve the teens in more active helping with story times or summer reading, or find ways to utilize their technical expertise, go for it!

Finally, if you are not sure if your library policies are fair, talk to the teens who use your library. They will let you know if they are aware of library policies that discriminate against them. As noted earlier in the chapter, their critical reasoning skills make them acutely aware of adult hypocrisy and injustice, so they will have noticed. At the same time, they are also learning to take responsibility for their actions, so asking them to help create the list of consequences for breaking rules will help to give them a sense of ownership and responsibility. This goes for the whole library, not just the teen space.

You may also want to consider having fewer rules, rather than more. The problem with having a lot of rules is that it encourages teens to find creative ways around them: "But the rules don't say that we can't stand on our heads on the tables!" Charlotte Mecklenburg Library in North Carolina has a teen space called "The Loft." Here are the rules for The Loft: Respect Yourself. Respect Others. Respect the Space.

What more is needed than that?

FUNCTION

Library spaces for teens should be flexible and should consider all the ways that teens want to interact with the library: studying, relaxing, visiting, listening to/viewing materials, making, using the computers and other devices. As we noted in Chapter 1, teens are used to working collaboratively, and, in fact, are often required to do so for school. Having a space that allows them to move tables and chairs together and apart as necessary acknowledges this need and gives them autonomy over their space and their work.

Seating

In a 2014 article for *Public Libraries*, Anthony Bernier and Mike Males presented their research on teen use of teen library spaces. Their findings emphasized the importance of various seating options in the creation of what teens considered a welcoming space. In their survey, "respondents reporting favoring group seating (such as couches, benches, or platform risers) over conventional individual or task seating. Large majorities wanted seating to be varied and moveable. And a surprising one-third expressed preference for sitting on or near the floor over all other options." Bernier and Males point out the need for young people to move and stretch their bodies and how this leads to a variety of postures both on standard seating and on the floor. Adults may object to these postures, but they seem natural to teens.

Standard four-chairs-to-a-table study seating can be overly restrictive to teens. Teens who are studying together, or even those who are watching younger siblings, may find it more appropriate to share a single chair.

Location and Sightlines

Ideally, a teen area should be separate from both the adult and children's sections of the library. Teens don't want to have to walk through groups of small children to reach their space, nor do they want to have their space adjoining an area where adults are trying to read or study. Teens do like to see who is coming and going, however, so a location that overlooks the main entry or most-used pathways in the library will be appreciated. However, the area should not itself be in the middle of normal library pathways. As noted earlier, teens enjoy sitting (or sprawling) on the floor, so ideally a teen area will be out of the way enough to allow them to do that without impeding traffic.

If there is no staff desk in the teen area, there should be ample sightlines into the space from staffed areas of the library. If a teen area is hidden away in a corner of the library, staff should not be surprised to find that teens will use the opportunity to engage in inappropriate behavior, from excessive public demonstrations of affection to minor vandalism.

Appearance

A teen space should be teen-friendly but not overly cute. The furnishings should be sturdy and washable. As noted before, furniture and seating should be flexible. A blank wall, a window, or solid shelving endcaps all provide space that can be utilized in teen programming, as noted in Chapter 4. If possible, have decorations (like posters) that are changeable, and change them frequently, so that the space does not get outdated.

CONTENTS

The contents of your teen space will depend greatly on the space available, and on the general collection policies of your library, as discussed in Chapter 3. At the very least, however, a dedicated teen space, no matter how small, ought to have some or all of the following:

- *Popular new teen books*. This may include both hardbacks and paperbacks of titles that "everyone" is asking for. Popular series and books that are being made into films are sure winners.
- *Nonfiction* on topics of interest to teens, from entertainment-related subjects to self-help.
- *Magazines*. Collect an assortment of magazines that are favorites of teens.
- *Audiobooks*. Although most teens will prefer to listen to audiobooks on their phones or other devices, having a small collection of audiobooks on CDs can serve as a reminder that the format exists. Post signs and instructions on how to use the library's download-able audio services.
- *Music*. As with audiobooks, teens download the vast majority of their music. If your library offers streaming or downloadable music services such as Hoopla, Freegal, or Alexander Street, make sure that the teen area includes signs and instructions on how to access these services.
- *Display space*. Space to display teen contributions can make the space really feel personal to them. A wall, a whiteboard, or a window can serve as a place to interact with teens and allow them to interact with one another. In addition, there should be display units for library staff to use to create displays of library materials. The displays should be changed frequently.
- *Computers*. Teens both want and need computer access. A teen space should have at least a few computers that are dedicated to use by teens.
- *Electric outlets*. Teens are heavy users of their devices, and by the end of the school day they will need to charge them. Ample electric outlets will allow them to do that without getting into fights with one another or other library users about access to power.
- *Chairs and tables*. As noted earlier, seating should be flexible and comfortable.

AN ENCOURAGING STORY

It is possible to grow a teen space over time. Librarian Charli Osborne, from Oxford, Michigan, tells how she grew her teen space from an alcove with two walls of shelving and four chairs into a 1,200 square-foot teen space with a 10,000-item collection over the course of about eight years. She collected circulation statistics, which ultimately led to getting a separate line-item in the collection budget. She began doing programming for teens, and as more and more teens used the library, they began to demand their own space. When an opportunity arrived to repurpose some space within the library, community surveys overwhelming demanded more teen space. By collecting and sharing statistics, ruthlessly advocating for teens, and getting teens engaged in the library's services, she was able to create a space where none had existed before (Flowers 2011, 50).

REFERENCES

Bernier, Anthony and Mike Males. July/August 2014. "YA Spaces and the End of Postural Tyranny." *Public Libraries* 53(4): 27–36.

Bolan, Kimberly. 2016. "YALSA Position Paper: Teen Spaces and Public Libraries." Rev. ed. Available at: http://www.ala.org/yalsa/sites/ala.org.yalsa/files/content/Position Paper_TeenSpaces_updated2016.pdf.

Flowers, Sarah. 2011. *Young Adults Deserve the Best: YALSA's Competencies in Action.* Chicago: ALA Editions.

Kuhlmann, L. Megan, et al. July 7, 2014. "Learning from Librarians and Teens about YA Library Spaces." Available at: http://publiclibrariesonline.org/2014/07/learning-from-librarians-and-teens-about-ya-library-spaces/.

YALSA. 2012. "National Teen Space Guidelines." Available at: http://www.ala.org/yalsa/guidelines/teenspaces.

CHAPTER 7

Speaking Up for Teens

Library services that are good for teens are also good for the library and good for the community. When teens have positive, empowering experiences in the library and with library staff, they learn to become more engaged. As teens are developing their identities, it is good for libraries if they also recognize the value of the library in the community. To do that, the library must support teens' needs and recognize their concerns, while also giving them opportunities to see themselves as part of the community. For their own sake and for the sake of our communities, it is best if today's teens become confident, competent, and caring adults. As adults and as community members, it is the obligation of library workers to speak up for teens, their needs, and their rights, and to empower them to do the same for themselves.

EQUAL ACCESS TO MATERIALS AND SERVICES

In the United States, the First and Fourth Amendments to the U.S. Constitution are the bases of the concept we call *intellectual freedom*. "Intellectual freedom" is a broad term that encompasses several ideas, notably the right to freedom of speech and the right to privacy. In library terms, this means that library users have the right to have access to information on all subjects from all points of view and that their access to this information should not be examined or judged by others.

Public libraries generally have policies that support free and equal access to library materials for all users. The Library Bill of Rights, originally adopted by the American

65

Library Association in 1939, states that "A person's right to use a library should not be denied or abridged because of origin, age, background, or views." A parent or guardian may impose restrictions on his or her own child's use of certain library materials, but the library's job is to have the materials available—not put barriers in the way of those who want to use them.

Library workers protect young people not by keeping information from them but by showing them how to evaluate information, think critically about it, and learn for themselves what materials meet their needs. Blocking access to certain types of materials or information based on our own comfort level may mean preventing teens from learning about things that are vital to their own development, growth, and well-being. As library staff, our job is to help teens find the materials best suited to their current information needs. For more background on ALA's position on access for minors, see "Free Access to Libraries for Minors" and "Access for Children and Young Adults to Non-print Materials." These are interpretations of the Library Bill of Rights pertaining specifically to children and teens and can be found on ALA's website.[1]

In practice, however, library policies and procedures may restrict a teen's ability to use the library. Examples are library cards for youth that limit their ability to check out materials from the adult collection and shorter time limits for the use of computers in the teen area. An unfortunately common practice that limits teen access is avoiding the purchase of certain materials out of a fear that some parents may find these materials inappropriate for their children. It is important to remember that teens vary widely in intellectual and emotional maturity and that families are different, too, in terms of their values and practices. Many factors influence these differences, including culture, socioeconomic class, and religion, but as library staff we should not be making collection decisions based on those factors. We should be creating collections that meet the needs of our users, and we should be finding ways to facilitate their access to our collections.

HANDLING CHALLENGES TO MATERIALS

So what do you do when someone challenges a book, magazine, video, or any other item that the library owns as inappropriate for teens? This is very likely to happen at some point, so it is useful to think about it ahead of time and to consider your own response. You should be aware of what your library's collection development policy covers and where you can quickly locate a copy. You should know whether the library has a collection development policy for teen materials. You should know whether your library has a certain procedure to be followed, or a form to be filled out, in the case of a challenge to library materials.

Here are some tips for dealing with challenges:

- Be polite and calm.
- Listen.
- Acknowledge the person's concern. ("I'm sorry you're upset.")
- Don't get defensive.
- Avoid library jargon.
- When possible, give facts and policies in writing.
- Ask questions. Find out what solution the person wants.
- Offer to refer the matter to your supervisor.

Here are some phrases you may want to keep in mind:

- We encourage you to visit the library with your children.
- We are happy to provide suggested reading lists for various ages.
- We're confident we have or can get materials that meet your needs.
- We would love to work with you and your child to find just the right book.
- Our goal is to provide the best possible service for teens, and we're proud of what we offer.
- Libraries offer a wide range of materials and not everyone is going to like or approve of everything.
- Our teen collection serves teens from 12 to 18, so not everything in it is for every teen. We encourage you to select books with your child or talk about the books with your child when he or she brings them home.

Don't assume that every parental complaint is actually an attempt to get a book removed from the library. Sometimes the parent is just feeling a bit lost and helpless and wants to vent. Often just listening is enough. If the parent or another adult actually wants the item removed from the library, or even moved to another collection in the library, provide him or her with the proper way to request that action. Some libraries have "reconsideration forms"; in other libraries the complaint might be referred to a supervisor or to the collection development librarian.

Remember: Challenges to library materials are not personal attacks on you. Stay calm and courteous and use appropriate ways to offer help.

PRIVACY

The library's main purpose is to facilitate access to information—not to monitor it. However, adults are accustomed to monitoring what children are doing in order to ensure their safety. Teens, as we have noted before, are not children, and their growing sense of self demands that we respect their privacy. As with access to materials, honoring a teen's right to privacy can be helped or hindered by the library's policies, procedures, and practices. The issue commonly comes up in circulation matters, especially when a parent wants to know what is checked out on the teen's card. Your library will have policies and procedures in place for dealing with these matters, and you should find out what they are.

When a teen approaches you with an information need, you should address the teen—and not direct your reply to anyone else who happens to be with them. Sometimes there may be a parent who may want to lead the conversation. Always ask your questions of and direct your replies to the teen. Although this may not seem like a privacy issue, since the parent is standing right there, it says to the teen that you understand whose request you are dealing with. Teens who have been treated respectfully in this way are more likely to trust that they can come to you with requests of a more private nature in the future. Similarly, although many teens seem surrounded by friends, engage with them one-on-one whenever possible.

Teens can sometimes get very chatty with library staff, especially if they spend a lot of time in the library and get to know you well. It is easy to fall into the trap of "leaking" information to one of these chatty teens about what their peers are reading or working on. It may seem harmless enough to say, "Megan loved this book; you should try it," or "Oh, yes, I just helped Jason find some information on ancient Egypt, too," but it is best to restrain oneself. If Megan wants to tell her friend about the book, she will, and it's up to Jason to decide if he wants to share what he's working on with his classmates. There may be reasons that teens do not want to share that information, even with the best of friends, and rather than trying to guess which topics might be "safe," it is far better to refrain from sharing any information about what another user is reading or researching or even with whom he came to the library.

As someone who may be helping a teen find materials to read, listen to, or view, you should certainly ask questions, but be conscious of nonverbal cues. If a teen is standing in the stacks but avoids eye contact, turns slightly to the side as you approach, or otherwise gives off "leave me alone" signals, say something like, "Finding what you need?" as you pass by, slowing just enough to give the teen a chance to say "no" while conveying that a "yes" answer is perfectly fine. This lets a self-conscious teen know that you are available to help but are not judging what he is doing.

Another simple tip for respecting teens' right to privacy is to give them some (physical) space. Some teens, especially boys, may find it difficult to have even a straightforward conversation about books in a face-to-face setting. These teens may be more comfortable sharing their thoughts and ideas if you are standing next to them instead of in front of them. If you are looking at the books and library materials instead of directly at the teen, he or she may find it less intimidating and invasive. Again, watch for nonverbal cues to help you determine the best approach.

COMPUTER USE AND FILTERING

The Internet has vastly changed the way libraries operate. Now many teens come to the library primarily (or only) to use the computers, even if they have computers and online access at home. The library can be a place to use computers in a social setting.

Here again, library policies and procedures can affect the access that teens have to information. Although the American Library Association does not recommend filters on computers in publicly funded libraries, many communities have decided that unlimited access to the Internet is harmful in a public setting and have installed filters. In many cases, these block access for minors to sites that the filtering software deems inappropriate. If your library uses Internet filtering, you should know how it is used and what your library's policies are regarding Internet use. If a teen is doing research on a topic and finds a site blocked, is it permissible (or even possible) for library staff to unblock it? If there are unfiltered computers in the adult area, are teens permitted to use them? You must, of course, enforce your library's policies, and you will be in a better position to do so if you know what the policies are and why they exist.

Online Privacy

Library staff can have a major role in helping teens to navigate the web and evaluate the content found there, as well as helping teens learn the rules of online safety. Teens have grown up online, and they may have a hard time grasping the fact that nothing online is truly "private." For an excellent, brief illustration of the way a teen's online identity lingers over the years, watch the video "Identities" from the Berkman Center's Digital Natives project (based on the book *Born Digital*, by John Palfrey and Urs Gasser).[2] We can help teens be aware that what they post online is not necessarily visible only to "friends." They may be shocked to learn that college admissions officers and potential employers are using the web to check out applicants.

Behavior

Another issue that comes up about Internet use is the behavior of teens while they are using library computers. As we have seen, teens are social beings, and they like to operate in groups. This can result in loud conversations, giggling, and other noisy and disruptive behaviors. Library policies that limit the number of people at a computer may seem reasonable in terms of keeping the noise level down, but they work against the desire and the developmental need of teens to have feedback and reinforcement from their peers.

Enforce rules fairly; don't discipline teens for talking too loudly at the computers if you aren't doing the same with the moms who are talking outside the story hour room or the seniors who are discussing their investments in the newspaper reading area. Bear in mind what we discussed in Chapter 2 about behavior issues. Give them warnings: "Control your voices, or you will have to leave." Give them options: "You can keep the noise level down, or some of you can leave and take the conversation outside." Bear in mind that teens are naturally self-centered and telling them they are disturbing others in the library may not mean much to them. Instead, focus on what they want: to use the computer. If they want to continue to get their computer time, they must obey the rules of the library.

Tip: Be polite, direct, and—most of all—consistent in enforcing behavior rules.

Teens' right to privacy extends to what they are viewing on the computer. No matter what you suspect they are viewing (from the giggling and screeching that's going on), deal with it as a behavior issue. As you walk up to them, look at the teens, not at the screen, and ask, "Are you finding the information you need?" Your presence will often be enough to cause them to quiet down and to navigate quickly to another website. In any case, deal with what is really causing the disturbance—the noise. If another library user complains about what a teen is viewing on the computer but there is no disturbance, you may not need to do anything at all. Thank the other person for their concern but don't promise that you will stop the teen. You may want to go up to the teen and remind him or her that he or she is in a public place and that others can see what he or she is viewing.

Sometimes the complaints from other library users come when they see that teens are playing games or using chat on the computers. They may want you to "tell those kids to stop playing, so people can use these computers for real work." A teen's use of the library computer for games and social networking is no less "real" than any adult's use of the computer for checking auctions on eBay, looking at pictures of grandchildren, or, yes, social networking. Teens have the same right as adults to use library computers for whatever they want during their allotted time. When we recognize teens' rights to be there, to use library resources, and to be treated with respect, we are modeling that behavior for the whole community.

OTHER ETHICAL ISSUES

Part of the library's role in supporting information literacy for teens involves helping them understand that not everything on the Internet is free of cost and freely available for them to use. Teens are accustomed to seeing and creating projects that involve music, photos, videos, and other media, and they usually think (as do many adults) that they can just go onto the Internet, download something, and pop it into their project. They may not even realize that it is plagiarism to cut and paste an article from the web into a paper without acknowledging the original author. Library staff should understand the basics of copyright for themselves, and staff should show teens how to cite sources and how to find legally available materials to use in their projects. Library staff should also model ethical behavior in our own use of music, movies, pictures, and other media in library programs and services. Showing them how to find royalty-free images such as those with Creative Commons licenses (www.creativecommons.org) is a way to help them use the Internet ethically, while also protecting their own intellectual property.

ADVOCATING FOR TEENS

You have a personal and/or professional interest in providing library service to teens, or you wouldn't be reading this book. The next step is taking the message about excellent library service for teens and sharing it. In order to provide the best possible service to teens, everyone needs to be on board: all library staff members, the community's leaders, and, in fact, the whole community.

This doesn't have to be complicated. Sometimes advocacy just means reminding another staff member that teens are people, too, with the same rights to use library resources as adults or children. Sharing information about teens that you have learned from this book—or from working directly with teens—can help demystify teens to other library workers who may not be used to dealing with them. Advocacy can also extend beyond the library, to spreading the word to others in the community about what the library has to offer teens.

Library staff, especially those who work directly with users, are in a perfect position to spread the good word about teen services, as long as they are provided with the proper tools. Everyone in the library should know if there is a teen program coming up, what it is, and where to find more information about it. Circulation desk staff can share the information with teens and parents who are checking materials out, and teenage shelvers and volunteers can pass the message along to their friends.

You can also advocate for teens among your own friends and acquaintances. They probably already know you work in the library, but they may be surprised to find that you are working with teens. A lot of people think that teenagers don't even come to the library ("Aren't they spending all their time on their devices?"). Simply sharing a story about a good library experience you had with a teen (maintaining confidentiality, of course) can change someone's ideas about what teens are like. Your positive attitude and enthusiasm about serving teens is the best possible advertisement.

And teens can advocate for your library, too. For some really great examples of this, take a look at the Teen Advocacy Video Project (https://www.youtube.com/play list?list=PL6CC681DE97AC97A4) created by teens at the Charlotte Mecklenburg Library explaining what the library means to them. The best testimonials demonstrate the importance of keeping library branches open, preserving staff, and offering hours that fit into teens' schedules, such as evenings and weekends. Hosted on YouTube, the videos will be shared with elected officials, adult community members, and a Future of the Library Task Force charged with making library funding sustainable despite the current economic climate.

You never know who you are going to meet in your community, and it is always a good idea to be prepared to talk about what you do and how important the library is. Most community members are aware of the library as a resource for children, and they love to hear about story times and summer reading clubs. However, many may not be aware of the kinds of programs and services libraries offer for teens. Do they know that teens are volunteering in your library every day after school? Do they know that teens are gaining leadership skills by participating in the library's teen advisory board? Do they know that teens are creating podcasts or reviewing books for the library's website? People are all too used to hearing negative stories about teens; this is your chance to share positive stories about teens and get in a plug for the library at the same time. See the YALSA Advocacy Toolkit (http://www.ala .org/yalsa/sites/ala.org.yalsa/files/content/Advocacy%20Toolkit.pdf) for more suggestions of ways you can advocate for teen services.

Elevator Speeches

One good way to advocate for teen services is to have in your head one or two "elevator speeches" on the topic of teens and libraries. An elevator speech is a short statement that sells an idea in the time it takes to ride the elevator to your floor, in other words, about 30 seconds or less (or about 90 words). It should be a concise, punchy description that highlights the value of your idea. In thinking about an elevator speech, consider how you might advocate for programs, services, or resources for teens in your library. Think about whom you would like to run into (mayor, city manager, a library trustee, any community member, a possible funder for library programs, etc.), and then consider these tips:

- Tell the listener how these programs, services, or resources benefit teens in your community.
- Give a concrete, interesting example.
- Consider: what are you trying to do, and why is it important?
- Be creative!

The Association for Library Service to Children (ALSC) has a great initiative called Everyday Advocacy (http://www.ala.org/everyday-advocacy/speak-out/elevator-speech) that includes very specific tips and a great infographic on creating an elevator speech aimed at advocating for young people in the library.

Advocating in the Community

Here are some ways you can advocate for teens in your community. Most of the time, advocacy just involves spreading the word about positive things that are going on with teens and the library.

- Provide your local newspaper, radio station, or TV station with news releases about upcoming library events, such as summer reading, a major program, or events like Teen Read Week and Teen Tech Week. YALSA provides sample news releases and public service announcements for these events, so all you have to do is plug in your specific information.
- Most city councils and county boards of supervisors regularly issue proclamations that highlight events or organizations. Again, Teen Read Week and Teen Tech Week are good times to issue proclamations, and YALSA provides templates.
- Also, city councils and county boards of supervisors normally have public comment sessions before their regular agendas. This is an opportunity for any member of the community to speak to the council or board for three minutes or less. Coordinate with your library director to make occasional visits to your governing board to report on good things that the library is doing with teens.
- Invite your city councilors, county supervisors, and state and federal representatives to library events, such as the summer reading wrap-up or a major teen program. Elected officials love to have their pictures taken in the community doing things that are positive and fun. Even if they don't come to your events, by inviting them, you are making sure that they (or their staff) know about things that are happening in the library.
- Send thank-you notes. If a community partner helps you with a library program (by providing food, services, or money), send a thank-you note. If an elected official shows up for a library event, send a thank-you note. If a teacher offers her students extra-credit to attend a library program, send her a thank-you note. If the Friends of the Library provide funds for a program, send them a thank-you note. In your thank-you notes, include comments from actual teens whenever you can.

NOTES

1. http://www.ala.org/advocacy/intfreedom/librarybill/interpretations. Other interpretations to the Library Bill of Rights that may be of interest to those who work with teens are "Internet Filtering," "Minors and Internet Activity," "Restricted Access to Library Materials," and "Labeling Systems."
2. http://blogs.harvard.edu/youthandmediaalpha/publications/videos/borndigital/. In addition to the video on "Identities," the blog contains other videos about teens and their online presence, including ones on privacy, safety, activism, and more.

REFERENCES

ALA. "Library Bill of Rights." Available at: http://www.ala.org/advocacy/intfreedom/librarybill.

ALSC. "Write an Elevator Speech." Available at: http://www.ala.org/everyday-advocacy/speak-out/write-elevator-speech.

YALSA. 2013. "YALSA Advocacy Toolkit." Available at: http://www.ala.org/yalsa/sites/ala.org.yalsa/files/content/Advocacy%20Toolkit.pdf.

CHAPTER 8

Teen Volunteers and Workers

Libraries can provide many opportunities for teens to gain work experience, both as volunteers and as paid workers. In this chapter, we'll look at some of the ways teens can help in your library, and why you might want them to.

TEEN VOLUNTEERS

When considering teen volunteer programs, it is important to think about both what the library will get out of it and what the teens will get out of it. So let's start with the library. Why would you want to have teen volunteers?

The Library's Reasons

- For the help they can give. It seems as if there are always little jobs in the library that you don't have time to do. We'll discuss later in this chapter what some of those jobs might be.
- To get to know the teens in the area. Working one-on-one with another person is always a good way to get to know them better. Having teen volunteers is a way to create relationships with an important library constituency, and teen volunteers can be a great source of feedback on your teen collections, services, and spaces.

- Provide help that teens are requesting. Many schools today require their students to do a certain number of service hours per semester, and the library can be a source of those hours.
- To create advocates for the library and the community. Teen volunteers learn more about the library and its role in the community. They can then, in turn, share that information with their families and friends.
- To provide role models for younger teens and children. Many teen volunteers help out with children's crafts and programs, and doing so allows both children and their parents to see teens in a positive and helpful light.
- To curb bad behavior. Volunteering not only can keep them busy when they might otherwise be causing trouble, but it can create a sense of ownership in them. As a result, they take the initiative to curb bad behavior in other teens in the library.

The Teens' Reasons

And why would teens want to volunteer in the library? What's in it for them?

- To get community service hours for school. As noted, many schools require service hours, and the library can be a place to perform those. The library may be a familiar place for teens and somewhat less scary than a homeless shelter or food bank.
- To have opportunities for social activity with friends. Teens may volunteer together with their friends. Having a specific activity they can do together can be fun.
- To share their expertise and skills. Many teens have strong creative, technical, or artistic skills that can be of use in library programs and services. Sharing those skills validates the teen's worth in the community.
- To have something for their college applications. Volunteering (and working) in the library is a positive activity for college applications. It shows involvement in the community and a sense of responsibility. In addition, some particular incident may provide the basis for a college application essay.
- To have leadership opportunities. Especially since it is harder than ever for teens to find paying jobs these days, volunteering can provide leadership opportunities that they don't have elsewhere. A volunteer opportunity such as working with other teens, or with children, gives teens a chance to learn some of the basic tools of leadership.
- To have an opportunity to work with adult mentors. Teens need to have good relationships with nonparent, nonteacher adults, and libraries provide a place where that can happen. A volunteer program gives teens the chance to work specifically with one or more adults and also the chance to meet the other adults who work in the library.

The Reasons Not to Have Volunteers

Volunteers can be help, but it is not necessarily "free" help. Having an effective volunteer force, whether it is composed of teens or adults, means work for the library staff. Volunteers need to be trained, scheduled, mentored, supervised, and occasionally disciplined. Volunteer jobs need to be decided on, and the materials and space needed to perform them need to be provided. Someone needs to keep track of volunteer jobs and the hours that individual volunteers spend doing those jobs. Volunteers do not always take their responsibilities seriously and do not always do their jobs exactly the way library staff would like them done. In a library that has employee unions, there may be strict limits on the types of jobs volunteers are allowed to do. Teens in particular can be negligent about showing up at the times and days scheduled. We'll discuss all of these problems and how to deal with them later on in the chapter.

VOLUNTEER JOBS

The following volunteer jobs are examples of the types of things a teen volunteer should be capable of doing. Whether you use teen volunteers for these jobs in your library depends on many factors, including the amount of space you have, the number of volunteers, whether you have adult volunteers doing some of the jobs, whether you are in a unionized environment, and more.

If your library workers are in a union, check the union agreement before assigning volunteers. Some unions do not allow volunteers to do work that is part of a union member's job description. Examples might include shelving, checking materials in or out, and reading stories to children.

- Clean computers and mice
- Cut scrap paper
- Fill pencil cups and scrap paper holders
- Cut images for flannel boards
- Cut paper to prepare for children's crafts
- Test out children's crafts
- Setup/cleanup program room
- Sharpen pencils
- Put magazines in order
- Put audio books in order
- Straighten shelves
- Search for books on "trace" or for holds
- Shelf read
- Dust shelves
- Fill displays
- Help create displays, bulletin boards, decorations
- Make signs and posters for upcoming events
- Remove "new" stickers from book spines
- Clean book covers
- Contribute to teen blog, YouTube, or Facebook pages
- Create and post book trailers
- Run DVD cleaning machine
- Help out during children's programs
  - Help children with crafts and activities
  - Take pictures
  - Keep count of participants
  - Help with sign-in
  - Run games and activities
  - Wear character costumes
  - Serve snacks

- ◦ Put on performances (puppet shows, readers' theater, etc.)
  - ◦ Hand out prizes at the end of summer reading
- "Book buddies." Read with kids. Help emerging readers maintain their reading skills over the summer by reading to them and having them read out loud.

THE PRACTICAL DETAILS

Running a volunteer program is a lot of work, and it takes both advance planning and continued attention. Volunteers must be recruited, vetted, scheduled, trained, supervised, and thanked.

Recruitment

How much recruiting you will need to do depends on your situation. If you have teens breaking down your doors to volunteer, you won't have to go looking for more. But you may need to recruit for specific times or specific jobs. Before you start to recruit, think about how many volunteers you will need as well as how many hours per week and how many weeks you will need them to work. Be sure also to consider your ability to supervise the volunteers. If you or another staff member can't supervise at the times and days the teens want to volunteer, it could pose problems.

For actual recruitment, consider starting with the teens who are already using the library. Ask them if they would be interested in doing some volunteer jobs for you during the hours when they are normally in the library. If you need to go beyond that, post a volunteer sign-up form on your library's web page or Facebook page. If the local schools require service hours, be sure that the service coordinator has your contact information, as well as details about the kinds of volunteers you need, and your requirements.

Vetting Volunteers

You may or may not be in a position to pick and choose among your volunteer hopefuls. In any case, it is a good idea to make the process of choosing volunteers as formal as possible, without being overly legalistic. Have your volunteers fill out an application or intake form. This serves two purposes: it gives you information about the volunteer, and it impresses upon them the seriousness of the commitment. Sample intake or application forms can be found at the end of this chapter.

Scheduling Volunteers

How you schedule your volunteers depends upon several factors, including how many volunteers you have, how many volunteer jobs you have, what kinds of volunteer jobs you have, what the volunteers' availability is, and what your availability is to supervise them. You can create a schedule with empty slots and ask your volunteers to sign up for the slot(s) they want. Or, you can ask them for their availability and then create a schedule based on that. If you ask for their availability, have them be as specific as possible: Monday and Wednesday afternoons between 2 p.m. and 4 p.m., for example.

Be specific from the beginning about how often and for how long they can or should volunteer. For example, let them know in your first discussion with them that once they commit to a volunteer shift, they will be expected to show up for that shift every week (or month or whatever) for an agreed-upon period of time. Even if they are trying to work only 20 hours of community service as fast as possible, you need to set the expectations for when they will show up and how long they will work.

You might want your volunteers to agree to work 2 hours every week for at least 10 weeks, for example. Or, if you have long-term volunteers, you can discuss with them how often you will entertain a discussion about changing their hours around.

Training

Training for volunteer jobs should be fast and fun. Don't make them regret signing up by going into a lengthy discussion about every aspect of their volunteer job. Your training session should include a general discussion (and written list) of basic guidelines and expectations. This doesn't have to be complicated. Common basic guidelines and expectations include:

- Show up for your scheduled shifts on time.
- Notify the library [specific person, phone number, e-mail] if you are not able to make one of your shifts.
- Be courteous to library staff, other volunteers, and library patrons.
- Do not use your cell phone during your shift.
- Respect patron privacy.
- Follow the library's dress code. [Note: this is something that the library will have to decide on. For example, if the volunteer is handling books or book carts, open-toed shoes may not be allowed.]
- Ask questions if you don't know what to do.

If this is their first volunteer job, teens may be unaware that they are actually expected to show up regularly and do the job. You can point out to them that this is good practice for when they get a paying job, when their paycheck will depend on such things!

Other topics for a training session could include:

- Show how the scheduling process works. Show them where the schedule is posted, and describe what to do if they want to change shifts with another volunteer.
- Show where they are to sign in and out, and record their hours.
- Introduce the volunteers to key library staff, including any staff who will directly supervise their work. If possible, introduce them to the library's director and other managers.
- Describe and demonstrate basic job duties. If you are having them do shelving, make certain that they understand the basic rules of library alphabetization (dropping leading "A"s and "The"s in titles, where to put "Mc" names, what to do with numerals, etc.) as well as the Dewey Decimal System (or whatever classification system you use). One way to approach this with teens is to turn it into a speed competition: who can alphabetize a cart of DVDs fastest, with fewest mistakes?
- Show them where to find their job assignment for the day. Does this need to be told to them by the volunteer supervisor, or is there a list posted somewhere?
- Show them where to find whatever supplies they need to complete their assignment for the day.
- Give them a library tour, and include things like where they should put their belongings, which bathroom they should use, and so on.

Managing Volunteer Jobs

Keep a running list of volunteer jobs. This will allow you to make a quick decision about where to assign any volunteer who shows up to work. Encourage other staff members to send you lists of projects that they could use teen volunteers for. Be sure to determine whether these jobs need the supervision of the requesting staff member, or whether they are something you can assign at will.

For some jobs, like dusting shelves, shelf-reading, and others that need to be repeated on an ongoing basis, it is a good idea to keep a chart or checklist for you and your volunteers to refer to. So, for example, if you need to send a volunteer out to dust shelves, you will know that the last volunteer dusted the fiction shelves from A to C, so your volunteer needs to start at D.

Maintain a binder with notes and instructions for regular jobs. You can refer your volunteers to the binder if they need to know how to do a job they've never done before. The binder should include information about where to find the necessary materials (dust cloths, paper to be cut into scrap paper, scissors, etc.). This will not only free you up from having to explain the same things over and over again, but it will empower your teen volunteers and let them know that you have confidence in their ability to work things out for themselves.

Supervising Volunteers

Even with the best volunteers and your best intentions, problems may arise in running a volunteer program. Start by making sure that your expectations and instructions are clear. Check the work of your volunteers, especially when they are new, and point out to them when there are things you would like to see done differently. Make this a conversation, not a lecture. Explain why you need to have things done a certain way but entertain suggestions if they have a better idea for how to accomplish a task.

As you work with your volunteers, observe their strengths and weaknesses and refine their volunteer assignments accordingly. Your super-creative teens will be much happier working on a display or bulletin board than cleaning computer screens. Teens who are more outgoing will be natural choices for helping out at children's programs, while those who are more shy and quiet will be perfectly happy in the back room, preparing materials for that program.

Sometimes, however, discipline is necessary. You will need to talk to the volunteer who is chronically late, who cancels at the last minute, or who regularly fails to show up. You will need to explain the library's expectations again and make it clear to them that their failure to follow through affects others. In addition, this is a good time to point out that these types of expectations are normal in the workplace. Be clear about the consequences for repeated absences: inability to complete their required service hours in time; inability for you, as the supervisor, to give them a recommendation for a job or college applications; necessity for you, as the supervisor, to have a conversation with their teacher or parents; necessity to end their volunteer stint with the library.

Other issues may arise among volunteers who show up regularly and even do good work. There are those, for example, who find it difficult to stay on task—they spend their entire shift wandering around talking to other volunteers, staff, or patrons. This may be solved by making sure that you schedule this person on different shifts from their friends, or by assigning the teen to a task that requires him or her to sit near you. Or, perhaps this is the teen who needs to be scheduled to help children with crafts or help seniors with technology.

In general, as with dealing with teen patrons in the library, give them second (and third) chances. Remember that their maturity can vary from day to day. Each day that they show up to volunteer should be a clean slate.

Volunteer Appreciation

Even if your volunteers are there specifically to fulfill a school service hour obligation, you should make sure they know that they are appreciated. How you do this will vary depending on the size and length of your volunteer program. If you have a regular group of teen volunteers, you may want to have a yearly volunteer appreciation party. If you tend to have more short-term groups (those who just volunteer in the summer, for example, or those who volunteer for three-month stints during the school year), you could consider having an appreciation event at the end of the term. Here are some suggestions for ways to thank your volunteers:

- Have a party. Invite all your teen volunteers, as well as staff who have worked with them. Have food and give each volunteer some sort of appreciation gift (see next for suggestions).
- Make T-shirts for your volunteers. Give these out at a party or when a volunteer has reached a certain number of volunteer hours.
- Offer small gifts such as bookstore gift cards, iTunes or Amazon gift cards, thumb drives, candy, movie passes or RedBox gift cards, and pizza coupons.
- Give them the option to exchange volunteer hours for library fines or fees.
- Buy a book for the library in their honor. Put a bookplate with their name on it in the book. Try to pick a book that matches their interests in some way.
- Give them a shout-out on your Facebook page. Have a "Volunteer of the Week" or "Volunteer of the Month" or simply list their names as a general thank-you for volunteers.
- Make certificates for them.
- Offer to write a letter of recommendation for a job or college application.

TEEN WORKERS IN THE LIBRARY

Teen volunteers may eventually become paid workers in the library. Many libraries hire teenagers to work as part-time shelvers or pages. Experience as a volunteer may inspire a teen to apply for one of these jobs. Having teen workers in the library can be an advantage for both the worker and the library.

Teen workers have the opportunity to learn valuable skills for the workplace. These range from the importance of following a schedule and showing up when assigned to doing a variety of jobs, from sorting and shelving to minor circulation tasks. In addition, working in the library gives teens the chance to learn about the organization and care of library materials, and about the larger picture of library service to the community.

When you include teen workers in the library's staff meetings you can share information about the library's philosophy and ethics. Teaching—both directly and by example—about the importance of patron privacy, about the value of customer service, about intellectual freedom, and about the role of the library in the community helps create informed citizens and ambassadors for the library.

Teen workers can also serve as an ad hoc teen advisory board. They can offer suggestions for purchase and ideas for programs. An engaged cohort of teen volunteers and teen staff can be your best promoters for teen programs and services. Teen workers and volunteers can help you keep up to date on the latest trends in the world of teenagers, which will in turn make you better able to provide the materials and services they want.

It is important to be aware of the special laws and regulations that apply to teen workers. Your state may have limits to the number of hours, the number of consecutive hours, or the specific hours (e.g., not after 8 p.m.) that a teenager may work. Teens themselves may not be aware of all of these limitations, so it is the responsibility of the library to know the laws and make sure they are enforced within the library.

LOOKING TO THE FUTURE

Teen volunteers and teen workers are natural pools from which to recruit future librarians and library workers. One of the developmental tasks of teens is to explore the world and start to consider what kinds of careers they may want as an adult. Teens who are volunteering or working in the library have a unique opportunity to see the kinds of work that librarians do. They are aware, unlike many members of the public, that librarians are not sitting at a desk reading all day but rather are performing a variety of jobs, including reference, readers' advisory, materials selection, program development, community involvement, and more.

Working in a library environment also teaches teens about some of the larger philosophical issues that libraries deal with: privacy, intellectual freedom, diversity, social responsibility, preservation, lifelong learning, and so on. These principles of librarianship may resonate strongly with teens who are searching for ideals. Teens with a strong sense of social justice as well as wide-ranging interests may find librarianship a perfect match. Having seen what libraries can do for society and for teens themselves can lead teens into a career in librarianship. And even if they do not become librarians themselves, former teen volunteers and teen workers often become strong advocates and ambassadors for libraries.

CONCLUSION

Managing teen volunteers and teen workers can be a challenge, and there may be times when you wonder if it is worth the trouble. But a strong teen volunteer program has so many benefits for both teens and the library. Teens learn library-specific skills, they learn to work as part of a team, and they make friends with other teens and with library staff and mentors. They have concrete work they can list on a college or job application. They develop self-confidence as they see what they accomplish. They feel good about helping others and making a difference in the community. The library gains experienced help to do some of the jobs that always needed doing. Even more, the library gains advocates and ambassadors.

Your Logo Here   # Teen Volunteer Application

Name (Print):_____Date of Birth: /__/__

Address / City/ State / Zip Code: _____

Teen Phone:_____Contact Email:_____

Parent/Guardian Name (Print):_____Phone:_____

Step 1. Which of the following tasks are you most interested in doing?

_____Shelving/Reading Shelves (Year-round)
Shelving is returning items to the shelves in correct order. Reading shelves is maintaining alpha and numeric order of the book collection.

_____ Event Assist
Teen volunteers assist the children's librarian with special programs and events, including setup, crowd management and clean up.

_____Teen Reading Buddy Program (Mondays Summer Only)
During June and July, Teen Reading Buddies help incoming 1st, 2nd and 3rd graders maintain their reading skills in a relaxed one-on-one weekly Monday reading time.

_____Reading Log Station (Summer Only)
During June and July, teen volunteers will help distribute summer reading forms, aide children & parents by logging their reading time, and distribute entry tickets for the end of summer drawings. Basic computer skills, laptop experience and attention to detail are helpful.

_____Building Assistance (Year-Round)
Assist library staff with general work such as dusting bookshelves, cleaning computer screens and keyboards, picking up materials left on tables, etc.

_____Clerical Assistance (Year-Round)
Assist library staff with work such as cleaning CDs and DVDs; assisting with photocopying, collating, and stapling documents; maintaining library bulletin boards; preparing crafts for library programs, etc.

Step 2. Please check below the day(s) of the week and the AM or PM shift that you are available to work.

	Mon.	Tue.	Wed.	Thu.	Fri.	Sat.
A.M.						
P.M.						

From *Crash Course in Young Adult Services* by Sarah Flowers. Santa Barbara, CA: Libraries Unlimited. Copyright © 2017.

STUDENTS AGE 14 AND OLDER

This is an opportunity for students who plan to apply for college admission, to earn community service hours.

During the school year, hours available are Monday to Wednesday 3:00 to 7:00 PM, Thursday 3:00 to 8:00 PM, Friday 3:00 – 6:00 PM and Saturdays 10:00 AM to 5:00 PM. Home Schoolers may volunteer during regular business hours. Summer volunteer hours expand to include shifts during regular business hours while school is out.

What we offer:

- Job related experience
- An opportunity to work with the public in a real world environment
- Verification of hours worked that may be used in certificate/portfolio/resume

What we require:

- A commitment of at least 2 hours per week or 36 hours per school semester. Students may only work a Maximum of 4 hours per day when working special events.
- Dependability. Please be punctual for your scheduled shift and call the circulation desk at xxx-xxx-xxxx if you are unable to work. Teens that are absent and have not notified the library will be noted as "absent without notification" on the volunteer schedule. More than 3 "absent without notification" will result in losing eligibility to volunteer that semester.
- Eligibility and extra-curricular activities. Volunteers participating in extracurricular activities must work a minimum of 2 out of 4 scheduled Saturdays during a month to remain active on the Saturday shift. Shifts can be made up by working a different shift day or doubling a Saturday shift. Staff must be notified of these schedule changes.
- Dress code: the library follows the prescribed campus dress code.
- Candidates will be required to attend a 2 hour orientation that includes library policy, handouts, a library tour and training. Volunteer schedules will be set at orientation and teens will earn 3 hours community service credits for attending orientation.

Teen application forms are available at the Library, and may be printed out from the Library's website.

For more information, please call the Volunteer Coordinator, at xxx-xxx-xxxx or email xxx@lib.org

I have read and agree with the above listed volunteer eligibility requirements.

Teen Applicant's Signature:_   Date:_____

I give permission for_____to volunteer on the day(s) time(s) noted on the application page.

Parent or guardian signature:_____Date:_____

Thank you for applying! We will call or email you within 5 business day to set up an interview.

From *Crash Course in Young Adult Services* by Sarah Flowers. Santa Barbara, CA: Libraries Unlimited. Copyright © 2017.

 **santa clara** county **library** district

Teen Volunteer Application
FOR AGES 14-17

Thank you for your interest in volunteering for the Santa Clara County Library District! The library welcomes teen volunteers and appreciates their contributions of time and talent to assist library staff in delivering services more efficiently and effectively. For information about teen volunteer options, please visit our Get Involved page or visit or call your local library. All library volunteers must be 14 years of age or older.

CONTACT INFORMATION	
Last name	
First name	Middle name
Address	
Email address	
Phone	Age
School	Grade

PREFERRED LIBRARY		
☐ Campbell	☐ Cupertino	☐ Gilroy
☐ Los Altos	☐ Milpitas	☐ Morgan Hill
☐ Saratoga	☐ Woodland	

YOUR AVAILABILITY

Please indicate when you would be available to volunteer in the boxes below.
Be as specific as possible — for example, in the box for Monday afternoon, you might enter "2–4 pm."
NOTE: The schedule of available volunteer work hours and minimum time commitments may vary by location. Contact your local Teen Librarian for details.

	Morning	Afternoon	Evening
Monday			
Tuesday			
Wednesday			
Thursday			
Friday			
Saturday			
Sunday			

FOR LIBRARY STAFF USE ONLY			
Date Received		Interview date	
Contacted by		Orientation:	

From Crash Course in Young Adult Services by Sarah Flowers. Santa Barbara, CA: Libraries Unlimited. Copyright © 2017.

 **santa clara**
county
library district

Teen Volunteer Application
FOR AGES 14-17

Do you need to complete these hours for school? If so, how many hours do you need and by what date do you need to complete them?

Why do you want to be a library volunteer?

Do you have any special skills that would be helpful at the library?

You may be assigned to one or more of the volunteer activities listed below. *Please note that all assignments may not be available at every location.* Libraries also have Teen Advisory Boards for which you can volunteer to work with the Teen Librarian and other teens to come up with programs and ideas to improve the library's services for teens. The Teen Advisory Board application process is separate - please contact the Teen Librarian at your local library for details. Please visit http://www.sccl.org/about/support-the-library/volunteer to learn more about these opportunities.

- **Building Volunteer**
  Assist staff with light cleaning such as dusting, cleaning computer screens and keyboards, or picking up items left on library furniture or floors.

- **Children's Services Volunteer**
  Assist staff with craft program preparations and other children's programs, sign up children for the Summer Reading Program, and perform other circulation and clerical duties in the Children's area.

- **Circulation Volunteer**
  Assist staff with sorting and shelving materials, straightening shelves, "shelf reading" shelves for accuracy, searching shelves for library materials, cleaning CDs and DVDs using a cleaning machine, performing minor cleaning and repair of library books.

- **Clerical Volunteer**
  Assist staff with photocopying, collating, folding, or stapling documents; help maintain library bulletin boards and publication racks; help prepare crafts or other items for library programs, assist with other special projects

- **Computer Volunteer**
  Provide tutoring to assist others in learning to use computers and common software applications.

I hereby submit my application to be a part of the fantastic group of volunteers that support the Santa Clara County Library District. I certify that every statement I have made in this application is true and complete to the best of my knowledge. I understand that any false or incomplete answers may be grounds for not selecting me or for dismissing me after I begin work. I understand that I will need to attend a mandatory orientation before volunteering, and that I may need to meet a minimum commitment of hours in order to continue volunteering.

Signature	Date

EMERGENCY CONTACT INFORMATION

Name	Relationship
Address	Cell phone
Home phone	Work phone

Please return your completed application to any Santa Clara County Library District location.

From *Crash Course in Young Adult Services* by Sarah Flowers. Santa Barbara, CA: Libraries Unlimited. Copyright © 2017.

CHAPTER 9

Keeping Up: Professional Resources and Development

By now, you have read this book and I hope you are excited about your role in serving teens in the library. But what comes next? How do you keep that excitement going? How do you continue to grow and learn about teen services in the library? In this chapter, I'll give you some resources for doing just that. You are in charge of your own professional growth and development. Reading this book is a step in the right direction, but there are many more things that you can do.

PROFESSIONAL ORGANIZATIONS

Joining one or more professional organizations is one of the simplest and best ways to contribute to your own professional growth. Your level of involvement in professional organizations can range from extensive to limited, but almost all of these organizations have collected many resources that can be extremely valuable, whether you are actively involved in the organization or not. Many of these resources, in fact, are even available to nonmembers.

American Library Association (ALA)

ALA (www.ala.org) is the oldest and largest library association in the world, dating back to 1876. ALA encompasses librarians and library workers from all types of libraries and all types of library specializations. ALA is the first place to look for information on libraries and for support for librarians, on everything from continuing education to book challenges. Within ALA, there are 11 divisions, each of which focuses on a different type of library or type of service, and numerous roundtables, each of which focuses on a narrow area of interest, and offices, which support the work of the association and its members. ALA is governed by an elected council, and by elected officers, who rotate on a yearly basis and is managed by professional paid staff, many of whom are librarians themselves.

Young Adult Library Services Association (YALSA)

YALSA (www.ala.org/yalsa) is one of the 11 divisions of ALA, and the one that focuses specifically on young adults (YAs), aged 12–18. In order to be a member of YALSA, you must first be a member of ALA. In most cases, you will be responsible for paying your own dues to become and remain a member of a library association. Yes, it can seem like a lot of money, especially if you are just starting out, but think of it as an investment in your career. If you don't care enough about your profession to become a member of the profession's associations, then who is going to care? Many of ALA and YALSA's resources are free for nonmembers, but to take the fullest advantage, it is worth it to join.

YALSA has around 5,000 members, of whom about a third are school librarians. YALSA's resources have featured prominently in this book, for the obvious reason that YALSA is the single national organization that is dedicated to helping those who serve teens in libraries. YALSA's mission is "to support library staff in alleviating the challenges teens face, and in putting all teens – especially those with the greatest needs – on the path to successful and fulfilling lives" (YALSA 2016).

To advance that goal, YALSA has, over the years, built up an extensive library of resources, all of which are available to members, and many of which are available to nonmembers. Some of the resources you should be particularly aware of are:

- National guidelines. YALSA has a library of national guidelines (http://www.ala.org/yalsa/guidelines) that have been developed by members and are available on the website. These include Core Professional Values, Programming Guidelines, Space Guidelines, Competencies for Librarians Serving Youth, and a Public Library Evaluation Tool, which allows libraries to gauge how well they are doing in meeting the competencies.
- *The Future of Library Services for and with Teens* (http://www.ala.org/yaforum/future-library-services-and-teens-project-report). This report was the result of a year-long grant-funded effort in 2013 in which librarians, educators, members of the non-profit and for-profit sectors, and experts in technology and adolescent development came together to discuss how libraries can best meet the needs of 21st-century teens.
- Position papers (http://www.ala.org/yalsa/guidelines/whitepapers/whitepapers). These are research-based papers on issues of interest and importance to those who work with teens in libraries. These position papers can help you understand the big picture of YA services, and they may be useful in persuading your library's director or board of trustees to make changes in order to support YA services better. The position papers include:
  - Adopting a Summer Learning Approach for Increased Impact
  - The Importance of a Whole Library Approach to Public Library Young Adult Services

- ◦ The Benefits of Including Dedicated Young Adult Librarians on Staff in the Public Library
- ◦ The Importance of Young Adult Services in Library and Information Science Curricula
- ◦ The Value of Young Adult Literature
- ◦ The Need for Teen Spaces in Public Libraries
- Online learning opportunities (http://www.ala.org/yalsa/onlinelearning). This includes courses, webinars, videos, chats, and online mentoring.
  - ◦ Online courses are offered occasionally on topics such as programming, readers' advisory, and technology.
  - ◦ One-hour webinars cover a variety of topics and are available free to members. In addition, webinars are archived and made available free to members and for a charge to nonmembers.
  - ◦ Badges. YALSA offers a virtual badge program that enables library staff members to gain knowledge and skills in the areas of YALSA's Competencies for Librarians Serving Youth.
  - ◦ YALSA's YouTube channel, YALSA Academy, contains short videos on topics of interest to YA librarians.
  - ◦ Virtual mentoring. On a yearly basis, YALSA's Virtual Mentoring program pairs an experience librarian with a new library worker or graduate student in library science.
- Journals. YALSA membership comes with an automatic subscription to *Young Adult Library Services* (*YALS*), a quarterly journal that features articles of interest to YA librarians. It is also available online to members. YALSA also has an online, peer-reviewed research journal, *The Journal of Research on Libraries and Young Adults* (*JRLYA*) (http://www.yalsa.ala.org/jrlya/).
- Toolkits and bibliographies (http://www.ala.org/yalsa/professionaltools). YALSA maintains a variety of toolkits and bibliographies, including those on:
  - ◦ Advocacy
  - ◦ Making in the Library
  - ◦ STEM Programming
  - ◦ Teen Interns
- Wikis (http://wikis.ala.org/yalsa/index.php/Main_Page). YALSA members maintain a number of wikis on areas of interest to YA librarians, including:
  - ◦ College and Career Readiness
  - ◦ Advocacy
  - ◦ Programming
  - ◦ STEM Resources
  - ◦ Teen Advisory Groups
- Electronic discussion lists. YALSA hosts a number of electronic discussion lists (http://www.ala.org/yalsa/professionaltools/onlineresources/emaillists#discussion). The most active of these are ya-yaac (young adult advisory councils) and yalsa-bk (book discussions). Discussion lists (listserves) can be a great way to virtually "meet" other YA librarians and get a real sense of the kinds of issues that are happening among other librarians who serve teens.
- Blogs. YALSA maintains two blogs. One, the YALSA Blog (http://yalsa.ala.org/blog/), is the official blog of YALSA and contains information about the association as well as articles of interest to anyone serving teens in libraries. The other, The Hub (http://www.yalsa.ala.org/thehub/), focuses on teen collections and includes content specifically

related to teen collections, including booklists, author interviews, and the occasional poll. Not only are the blogs a good source of information, but they provide opportunities for you to contribute to the profession. In addition to the normal posts for the blogs, beginning in 2017, The Hub will be the new home for YALSA's selected lists. Amazing Audiobooks, Best Fiction, Great Graphic Novels, and Quick Picks.

- Awards, grants, and scholarships (http://www.ala.org/yalsa/awardsandgrants/yalsaawardsgrants). Every year, YALSA offers nearly $200,000 in grants and awards to members. Some of this is in the form of sponsoring Spectrum Scholars and Emerging Leaders (programs of ALA) but much is direct grants to members who directly serve teens. These vary from year to year, but include collection development grants, grants for specific types of programming, and scholarships to attend conferences.

- Booklists and book/media awards (http://www.ala.org/yalsa/bookawards/booklists/members). As noted in Chapter 3, YALSA members select materials each year for a number of prestigious awards and lists. In addition, YALSA creates downloadable bookmarks and maintains the Teen Book Finder app (for Android and iOS) and a Book Finder database (http://booklists.yalsa.net/).

State and Regional Library Associations

Most states have their own state library association. In addition, there are several regional library associations that have membership from several states and/or Canadian provinces. These state and regional associations are smaller than ALA. Consequently, they are less expensive to join, and their conferences and activities are not as overwhelmingly large. It is often easier to get involved on a committee or other subgroup of a state library association. Many of the state and regional associations have youth-focused subdivisions.

Other Organizations

If you live in or near a major metropolitan area, there may be a local organization of youth-focused librarians. These are often just informal gatherings of librarians who work with teens. If there isn't such a group in your area, consider starting one. Gathering occasionally with other librarians who work with teens can be a very gratifying experience.

In addition to library-specific professional organizations, there are various education-focused groups that welcome librarian members. The National Council of Teachers of English (NCTE) (www.ncte.org) and its subset, the Assembly on Literature for Adolescents of the NCTE (ALAN) (www.alan-ya.org), are two of the notable ones. ALAN holds a workshop each year in conjunction with the NCTE annual conference that features YA authors and others in panels on YA literature. In addition, ALAN publishes a journal three times a year that features book reviews and articles about teaching YA literature.

Most states and many regions have reading councils or reading associations that offer conferences and newsletters for librarians and teachers. Search "reading association" and your state, county, or city name to find one near you.

JOURNALS

Reading professional journals is another good way to keep up with what is going on. Most membership organizations, like those aforementioned, issue journals. ALA's *American Libraries*, YALSA's *YALS*, and ALAN's *The ALAN Review* are examples. Some of the journals are moving to online formats, either in addition to or in place of print format.

Your library probably subscribes to one or more print journals that they use as selection sources. The most common ones are *Library Journal, Booklist, School Library Journal, Kirkus,* and *Publishers Weekly.* These are all good sources for reading reviews, which will help you with your selection as well as readers' advisory. But don't ignore the articles, which will often alert you to new trends in the profession.

The most helpful review journals for YA librarians are *Voice of Youth Advocates* (*VOYA*) and *School Library Journal,* which, despite its name, is not exclusively for school librarians. Both contain dozens of reviews in each issue.

School Library Journal (*SLJ*) (www.slj.com) has news and features about children's and YA services and has a column on Adult Books for Teens, which is also available online (http://www.slj.com/category/collection-development/adult-books-for-teens/). In addition, it has an extensive network of blogs, which we will discuss later in this chapter.

VOYA (http://voyamagazine.com/) is focused exclusively on services and materials for YAs. It has regular columns on programming, technology, science, graphic novels, and films, as well as other features and several online-only columns. *VOYA* reviews more YA books than any other journal, using its own unique P/Q rating system. Every book reviewed gets a "P" rating from one (lowest) to five (highest) based on the book's estimated popularity among teens and a "Q" rating from one to five based on the quality of the writing. Each year, the magazine creates a list of its "perfect tens"—books that got 5P and 5Q ratings during the past year. *VOYA* also creates several other booklists: The Nonfiction Honor List, Top Shelf Fiction for Middle School Readers, and Best Science Fiction, Fantasy and Horror.

BLOGS AND OTHER SOCIAL MEDIA

Reading a few blogs on a regular basis is a good way to keep up with what is going on in YA services and literature. Two that I mentioned before and that are extremely valuable are the YALSABlog (http://yalsa.ala.org/blog/) and The Hub (http://www.yalsa.ala.org/thehub/). Other blogs worth keeping an eye on are:

- Teen Librarian Toolbox (an SLJ blog) (http://www.teenlibrariantoolbox.com/). Book reviews, articles, programming tips, and more.
- Someday My Printz Will Come (an SLJ blog) (http://blogs.slj.com/printzblog/). Mostly active during the autumn months, this blog discusses and deeply examines books that are eligible for that year's Michael L. Printz Award for excellence in YA literature. This is one case where reading the comments can be just as helpful and enlightening as reading the blog posts.
- Heavy Medal (an SLJ blog) (http://blogs.slj.com/heavymedal/). Also mainly active in the autumn, this blog discusses books that are eligible for that year's Newbery Award.

Since the Newbery criteria include books for readers up to age 14, there is often quite a bit of discussion about books that could be considered YA books.

- We Need Diverse Books (http://weneeddiversebooks.tumblr.com/). Reviews, links, news, and general discussion about diverse books, in the widest possible sense.
- Reading While White (http://readingwhilewhite.blogspot.com/). Although often focused on children's rather than YA books, this blog takes a serious look at how we can all be "allies for racial diversity and inclusion."
- Stacked (http://stackedbooks.org/) has not only reviews of YA books but also articles and analysis about YA literature.

Many YA authors and advocates are quite active on Facebook, Twitter, and Tumblr. You can start by following YALSA on Facebook and Twitter, and their feeds will lead you to others you may want to follow.

WEBINARS

A variety of webinars are available online, many of them for free. They cover topics of all sorts relating to YA literature and services, as well as other library populations and services. In many cases, the webinars are available in archived form online. Here are some sources:

- YALSA (http://www.ala.org/yalsa/onlinelearning). As noted earlier, YALSA offers regular webinars, free to members, and for a fee to nonmembers.
- *Booklist* (http://www.booklistonline.com/webinars-archive). *Booklist* regularly offers free hour-long webinars. Often they feature representatives from publishers promoting their latest books and audiobooks.
- *School Library Journal* (http://www.slj.com/category/webcasts/) offers occasional free webcasts on topics related to children's and YA literature.
- WebJunction (http://www.webjunction.org/explore-topics/ya-teens/webinars.html) offers occasional hour-long webinars on topics related to YA services. Archived versions of past webinars are available.
- Infopeople (https://infopeople.org/training/view/webinar/archived). This continuing education project administered by the California State Library offers free webinars on all sorts of library-related topics, including YA services. Archived versions of the webinars are available.
- *Library Journal* (http://lj.libraryjournal.com/category/webcasts/) offers free webinars on a variety of topics, including occasional webinars on youth-related subjects. Webinars are archived.
- Demco (http://ideas.demco.com/webinars/). Demco offers occasional webinars on topics covering all areas of library work, including teen services.
- Texas State Library and Archives Commission (https://www.tsl.texas.gov/ld/online courses/index.html). Although some of the webinars are available only to Texas library staff, most are available to anyone who signs up and creates a (free) account. Past webinars are archived.

CONFERENCES

ALA, some of its divisions, and state and special library associations offer conferences on a regular basis. ALA has two conferences each year. The Annual Conference, usually held in late June, brings in over 20,000 librarians, vendors, and other interested people for a four-day conference that features speakers, continuing education workshops, celebrations, and a massive exhibit hall at which publishers and other library vendors display their wares. The Midwinter Meeting, usually held in January, is primarily a business meeting, meant to facilitate the work of committees. However, in recent years it has included more and more speakers and events to draw attendance. It is a smaller conference than the annual conference, usually drawing 10,000–15,000 attendees.

YALSA has conference sessions and other events at the ALA conferences and also offers a yearly Young Adult Services Symposium. Attendance is usually around 500, and all events and activities occur in one hotel. Since it is focused entirely on YA services and literature, and since it is relatively small, it is a good introduction to conference-going for the newcomer.

The Public Library Association (PLA) has a conference in even-numbered years. It focuses exclusively on public libraries and draws about 8,000 attendees. Like ALA conferences, it has a large exhibit hall with many publishers and other library vendors.

State and regional library associations usually have conferences every year or every other year. Some of these are quite large, others are more intimate.

Conferences can be expensive, so it helps if your library has a budget in place to allow employees to attend. Conferences can promote professional growth in four main ways:

- They provide useful sessions geared to specific interests. Experts in the field present talks or moderate panel discussions on best practices, success stories, and the latest trends.
- They provide opportunities for members to participate in the profession as committee members. The work of library associations is done by members. That includes selecting the winners of major awards like the Newbery, Caldecott, and Printz. It also includes writing documents like YALSA's guidelines and toolkits mentioned earlier, doing advocacy work, and much more.
- They provide opportunities for attendees to network with people from all over the state/country/world. It is easy to meet like-minded people at a library conference—at sessions, at after-hours events and receptions, even on the bus between conference hotels. Most library professionals are eager to share what it is they do, and some of the best learning can happen in one-on-one conversations.
- They provide opportunities for attendees to present conference sessions. Once you are a little more experienced, you can have the opportunity to present your own successes and knowledge at library conferences. The majority of speakers are other members, and if you have something to say, there are multiple venues for you to say it.

To get the most out of a conference, do your homework ahead of time. Plan out which sessions you would like to attend. You can focus on sessions that will help you in your current job, or those that will teach you new things and perhaps lead you to your next job. When you return home from the conference, consider writing up a report on the best sessions and speeches you attended and presenting it to your coworkers and/or supervisor. Supervisors are more likely to approve conference attendance if they see that you are learning, growing, and sharing information back at work.

Besides the actual conference sessions, conferences are a great opportunity to meet other library people who care about working with teens. Especially if you are a shy person, it can be difficult to get acquainted with strangers, but library professionals tend to be welcoming, friendly people, and it is really worth the effort to meet some of them. Here are some conference-going hints:

- Introduce yourself to those around you—in sessions, at receptions, on the shuttle bus. I actually have some good friends now that I first met by walking up to them at a conference reception and saying, "Hi, I'm Sarah!"
- In the exhibits hall, don't just grab all the free stuff—spend some time talking to the exhibitors. At the publishers' booths, spend some time looking at what they have on display, and when you get a chance to talk to one of the people staffing the booth, ask, "What's coming out that you're particularly excited about?" This gives them a chance to talk about their favorite book, and it might be one you've never heard of. You can also use the time to let them know what kinds of things the teens in your school or library are asking for.
- If a conference session doesn't interest you, go ahead and leave. Life's too short and there are too many interesting things going on to be bored!
- Sit in on some committee sessions. They are not all open to the public (award committees are closed), but many are. YALSA's Best Fiction for Young Adults sessions at ALA Midwinter and ALA Annual are always interesting, and once at each conference they dedicate one session to hearing comments on the nominated books from local teens. Other committees, including Great Graphic Novels and Children's Notables are also open. If you're interested in governance, YALSA Board meetings can be quite fascinating.
- Most of the divisions, including YALSA, have a "101" session at ALA Annual and Midwinter, which is intended to provide basic information about the division and about how you can get involved. These sessions are also great places to meet others, especially other new members.
- The divisions also have President's Programs and Membership Meetings, usually at the Annual conference, and these are also good places to meet people.
- YALSA usually has a "happy hour" at a local bar or restaurant. You don't have to be a member to attend, and it's a great place to meet up with other people who are interested in teen services. If you don't know what to say, just ask someone what they are reading!
- Be sure to take business cards. If you get a card from someone else, take a second to jot down on the card something about the person, to help you remember when you get home.
- If you can afford it, go to one or two paid meal events, like YALSA's Edwards Brunch. Or, if you are fortunate enough to get an invitation from a publisher or vendor to a meal, definitely take advantage. You never know who you might end up sitting next to, and how your jobs or lives might overlap. I was once at a luncheon where a librarian who wanted to know more about staff development models just happened to be seated with another librarian who does staff development as a full-time job. The two had a great discussion!

- In the weeks leading up to the conference, various ALA blogs, including YALSA's, will have a lot of helpful information. ALA and each of its divisions—and this goes as well for state and local conferences and symposia—has a local arrangements committee, whose job it is to tell you the best places to eat, the interesting places to visit, and so on.

YOUR PROFESSIONAL DEVELOPMENT PLAN

Creating a professional development plan for yourself is one way to make a commitment to your career. At least once a year, spend some time thinking about the skills and the knowledge that would help you become better at your job, or help you advance in your career. Then make some notes about how you could gain those skills or that knowledge. You might make a commitment to read a book, like this one, that fills a gap in your knowledge. Or you may decide that it would be a good idea to take a course, either online or in person.

Find out what kinds of continuing education and professional development are available to you and what your library might pay for. If you belong to a union, read your contract and find out if your union will reimburse you for classes related to your job. YALSA offers occasional online courses on teen services. Infopeople (www.infopeople.org) regularly offers four-week online courses covering a variety of topics, including youth services. These courses charge a fee. The Texas State Library (https://www.tsl.texas.gov/ld/online courses/index.html) also offers online courses in addition to webinars. Your state library may offer online or in-person courses or provide other types of training.

CONCLUSION

You are the person in charge of your career. If you want to gain knowledge, improve your skills, or expand your professional horizons, you are the one who needs to make that happen. Taking the initiative to participate in a professional organization like ALA, YALSA, or your state library association can help you build your career in various ways. In addition to providing you with information, such as the guidelines, toolkits, and webinars mentioned, these organizations offer you the ability to participate in leading the profession. Membership on committees can help you learn valuable skills in consensus-building, teamwork, and leadership—skills that will help you if you want to become a supervisor or manager.

Keeping up with the profession by reading journals and blogs and taking webinars and courses will give you knowledge that will help you have a voice in decisions that happen in your library. Increasing your knowledge about teens and teen services will allow you to be a voice for the teens in your community, and that in turn will help create a more vital, integrated community.

REFERENCE

YALSA. 2016. "About YALSA." Available at: http://www.ala.org/yalsa/aboutyalsa.

APPENDIX A

Creating a Crash Course Workshop

Now that you have read this book and are an expert on teen services at your library, you may want to consider giving a workshop on the topic to your coworkers or to parents in the community. Here are some suggestions for how to go about presenting a workshop based on the material in this book.

OUTLINE

Exactly what you cover is going to depend on several factors: your audience, their expectations, your time limit, your comfort level. But based on my experience, here is an outline of topics that library workers are usually interested in:

- Icebreaker
- Brain development
- Not children/not adults
- Distracting versus dangerous
- Approaches to teens
- Resources for collections and programs

You can cover this material in a half-day session, or expand it even longer. If you only have an hour or hour and a half, you can focus on brain development, distracting versus dangerous, and best approaches to teens.

GENERAL TIPS

As with any adult learning workshop, respect your audience. Don't create slides that are full of words and then read the slides to the participants. My approach in recent years has been to create slides that contain a large picture or illustration and a few words—five or six words per slide. Many libraries have uploaded pictures of their programs and displays to the web, but be creative in your illustrations.

There are a number of resources for royalty-free images on the web, and these can make your presentations lively and interesting. Try some of these sites:

- Morguefile (http://morguefile.com/)
- Freeimages (http://www.freeimages.com/)
- Creative Commons search (http://search.creativecommons.org/)
- Google images. When you do a Google image search, click on "Search Tools" and then click on "Usage Rights." You can limit your search to those items that are "labeled for reuse" or "labeled for noncommercial reuse."

Be sure to give credit to the creator(s) of the images you use. You can put an attribution on the page, or keep a running list that you include at the end of your presentation.

Allow some time in your presentation for audience participation. Depending on the audience size and space, you can do small-group work, or you can call for brainstorming suggestions from the participants that you record on a flip chart or white board or directly on the computer. I'll include some examples of audience participation activities later in this appendix.

To give your audience a break from your voice, show a short video or podcast to illustrate a point. I'll include some suggestions later on.

ICEBREAKER

I find it useful to begin workshops with some sort of icebreaker. It gives me an opportunity to learn something about the participants and for them to learn something about one another. A good icebreaker can also lead the participants into thinking about teens and teen services in a new and different way.

Books at 13 (or 15)

One of my favorite icebreakers to is ask participants to share about their favorite books when they were teenagers. If the workshop is focused on teens in general, or older teens, I might ask a question like, "What book rocked your world when you were 15?" If the workshop is focused more on younger teens (middle-schoolers, or even tweens) I might ask, "What were you reading for pleasure when you were in seventh grade?" I begin by sharing my own answers to these questions. Sometimes I even include pictures of my choices on a slide.

The answers to these questions can be quite illuminating and are a good lead-in to a discussion about the ways in which teenagers are still straddling the gap between childhood and adulthood. Some will talk about reading R.L. Stine while others talk about Stephen

King. Some will remember reading Judy Blume, while others will talk about Jacqueline Susann. The answers also show how reading interests vary depending on where the participant was raised: in the United States as opposed to another country; in an urban, suburban or rural environment, and so on. I find it moving to hear, for example, a Latina who recalls being stunned to discover *Bless Me, Ultima*, by Rudolfo Anaya, and to realize that there was literature for and by Latinos.

The titles that people mention show that anything and everything seems to qualify as a book for teens. Maybe the books have young protagonists, and maybe they deal with those important coming-of-age questions, but some are important because they have important ideas. They give teens a way to find out about something they were interested in, or to exercise their newly-attained skills in critical thinking and reasoning. They give them a way to experience something that either validates who they were or gives them insight into someone who is different.

A discussion like this can be a great place to start, because you can refer back to the responses as you talk about brain development, diversity, readers' advisory, and more.

Why Teen Services?

Another way to start a workshop on teen services is to get the participants to talk about why we serve teens in libraries. You can do this either as a whole-group brainstorming activity or divide the participants into smaller groups. Ask three questions and record the responses.

Start with: "Why do we serve children in the library?" People will generally be eager to talk about emerging literacy, sharing stories, school support, socialization, and more.

Then ask: "Why do we serve adults in the library?" Responses here will become more nuanced, as people will talk about adult needs for both recreation and information, as well as about the need to give taxpayers what they want and need.

Finally, ask: "Why do we serve teens in the library?" After having answered the previous two questions, this gives participants a chance to see how the answers to both cross over into the answers about teens. In fact, you can cross off the answers on your list of responses for both children and adults as you add them to the list for teens. There may be some unique responses in regard to teens, as well—encourage those and use them when you talk about teen developmental needs.

Generalizations and Diversity

One of the issues that sometimes come up when people think about teens is a tendency to lump them all together: All teens are noisy. All teens like graphic novels. All teens are disrespectful. Teens don't read. All teens are addicted to their electronic devices.

To break participants out of this mind-set, hand out pieces of paper and say, "Write down a list of words that describe you in some way." Give them a few minutes to make a list of attributes. Encourage them to think about ways in which they may be alike or different from others in the room.

Alternatively, divide the participants into groups of six or eight. Give them a sheet of paper and have them draw a flower on the paper; the flower should have one petal for each participant in the small group. Then have them discuss the ways in which they are similar and different. In the center of their flower, they should write down some attribute that they all have in common. Then each participant should take one of the petals and write on it some way in which he or she is unlike any other member of their group. Encourage them to avoid obvious physical characteristics and focus on experiences or more personal attributes.

BRAIN DEVELOPMENT

The information on brain development in Chapter 1 of this book is obviously a good place to start, as are the books and articles mentioned in the references to that chapter. This is often the most interesting topic for audiences, since most of them do not have a background in child or adolescent development and do not know anything about the latest research on the topic. If I have time, I find it useful to include an illustration of the brain, showing the different areas and their functions.

This is also a place you can include a short video. One that I have found useful and enlightening is a TED Talk by Dr. Sarah Jayne Blakemore on "The Mysterious Workings of the Adolescent Brain" (http://www.ted.com/talks/sarah_jayne_blakemore_the_myste rious_workings_of_the_adolescent_brain.html). Blakemore is a cognitive neuroscientist who studies the "social brain"—the areas of the brain that are involved in understanding other people—and talks about the way those areas are still growing and changing in teens.

Another option is to play a short podcast, such as one of those from the WNYC series "Being 12: The Year Everything Changes" (http://www.wnyc.org/series/being-12/). Some of the podcasts discuss research, such as "This is a 12-Year-Old Brain on Peer Pressure" or "Middle School: A 'Hot Mess' of Distractions." Others are interviews with young adolescents, talking about how they navigate this tough time of life.

NOT CHILDREN/NOT ADULTS

In this section, you can talk a bit about the ways in which adolescents are growing into their adult selves but are not consistently there. This is a good time to talk about their need for peer approval, their probable sleep deprivation, and their emotional volatility, and the difficulty they have in gauging the emotions or facial expressions of others (see Chapter 2).

A group exercise you can do here is based on Daniel Siegel's book *Brainstorm*. Siegel talks about four qualities of our minds that surface during adolescence: novelty-seeking, social engagement, increased emotional intensity, and creative exploration (Siegel 2013, 7). Ask the participants to brainstorm first positive and then negative aspects of each of the four qualities. This can be done in small groups or in one large group, using a flip chart or white board.

DISTRACTING VERSUS DANGEROUS

As discussed in Chapter 2, in dealing with teen behavior in the library it can be helpful to distinguish between distracting and dangerous behaviors. This is an opportunity to talk about the behaviors that require immediate and strong responses and those that can be seen as teachable moments.

An exercise you can do here is to come up with some scenarios from your own experience (like the incense-lighting I mentioned in Chapter 2) and have the participants discuss whether this was a distracting or dangerous behavior, and how they might have handled it.

APPROACHES TO TEENS

In addition to the brain information, this is the area that most audience members are going to be most interested in. Use some of the suggestions discussed in Chapter 2 under "Dealing with Teen Behavior" and "Dealing with Groups of Teens," and give examples of ways to talk with teens. Use examples from your own experience whenever you can—it will lend an authenticity to your words.

You can ask participants to share some of their troublesome experiences in the library with teens and have the group help brainstorm possible solutions. This is also a good place to get the participants to reflect on positive experiences they had with adults when they were teenagers; this will help them to see how their interactions with teens can resonate for years. Ask participants to take a few moments to consider the following:

- Think back to when you were between 12 and 18.
- What nonparent and nonteacher adult(s) had a positive impact on your life?
- What was it about them that you admired/respected/liked?
- Make some notes about their characteristics.

Then ask for two or three volunteers to share their experiences with the group.

RESOURCES FOR COLLECTIONS OR PROGRAMS

If you are presenting a workshop to library workers, they may be interested in having you share some resources for teen collections, programs, or both. Many of the suggestions in Chapters 3 and 4 lend themselves well to this type of presentation. For example, take some of the program suggestions in Chapter 4, find pictures to illustrate them, and share them with your audience. Sharing fun program ideas is a great way to get audiences engaged and thinking about things they can do in their own libraries. As much as you can, tie the program ideas back into the developmental assets and the needs of teens themselves.

CONCLUSION

Teens are often an underserved population in libraries. School librarians are becoming an endangered species, and in 2012, the Public Library Association's Public Library Data Services (PLDS) report found that only 37 percent of public libraries employed a dedicated young adult services librarian, down from 62 percent five years earlier (Agosto 2013). So the task of YA services has fallen on generalists. The more those of us who care about providing high-quality teen services in libraries share our knowledge, the better off our libraries and our teens will be. Even a small amount of information about adolescent development can change library worker's attitudes and approach to teens and make life a little easier for everyone in the library.

REFERENCE

Agosto, Denise. Spring 2013. "The Big Picture of YA Services." *Young Adult Library Services* 11(3): 13–18.

APPENDIX B

Programs

This appendix includes a little more detail on some of the programs mentioned in Chapter 4, as well as some additional program ideas.

BOOK CLUBS

Book clubs with teens can be a difficult proposition. Getting a regular group of teens to read the same book and come prepared to discuss it can be a challenge. But there are creative ways to have a successful teen book group.

Because teens like to express their opinions, but often don't like to be tied down, consider having a book club in which everyone is not required to read the same book. One way to do this is to have a genre book club, where everyone is reading fantasy books, or mystery books, or whatever, but not necessarily reading the same thing. When they come to the meeting, each member gets a chance to share what he or she has been reading and try to convince the other members to give it a try.

Another way to do the same thing is to have a "Smash or Trash" book club. Each member comes with a book that he or she has read and announces whether the book is a smash hit or is "trash." Over time, you can work with the teens to learn how to express what is good or not-so-good about a book, what works and doesn't work, and what is simply a personal preference.

If you have teens who are really interested in reading seriously and thoughtfully, you can have a Printz Award book club, in which they read books that are eligible for that year's Printz Award and hold their own Mock Printz discussions.

Some libraries have had a lot of luck with mother/daughter (or parent/child) book clubs. The mothers help to ensure that the teen girls actually read the books and show up. If any of your teens have read Heather Vogel Frederick's Mother-Daughter Book Club series of novels, they might be intrigued enough to give it a try. Book selections can alternate between young adult (YA) books and adult books of interest to teens, giving the parents a chance to read some YA books and providing a bridge for teens to read some adult books.

Finally, if you are going to have a book club in which everyone reads the same book, consider including some activities that are related to the book. That way, even if someone hasn't finished the book, they can still participate in the activity. Food is always popular, and if you can relate it to the book, so much the better.

BOOK PARTIES

Occasionally, a book will really strike the fancy of large numbers of teens, and it will seem like everyone is reading it. If the book is turned into a movie, the numbers will rise even more. We have seen this happen with the Harry Potter books and Hunger Games books, to mention two recent examples. When this happens, take advantage by hosting a party at your library using the book as a theme. Many libraries held Hunger Games events, in which there were various activities related to the books, like archery contests (with toy bows and arrows), spear contests (throwing a foam noodle at a target), fashion shows and makeovers, all based on events in the books. Be alert to the next fad book and get the teens to help you brainstorm activities related to it.

PERFORMING

If your teens are basically hams, put that to work for you and have them create performances for other library users. Your teens, for example, could do a series of skits and readings for the younger kids at a Summer Reading wrap-up party. Here are some suggestions for activities:

Readers' Theater

Your library's children's section probably has books with plays for readers' theater. It doesn't matter if the stories are a little young for teens, if they are going to present them to younger children. You can also find free readers' theater scripts online. The great thing about readers' theater is that it doesn't require a lot of preparation. Let the teens get together and choose their script, and go over it once or twice, and they're good to go, since they are reading the parts.

Poetry

Nonsense poems and narrative poems make great read-alouds. You can have teens choose poems and read them alone or work up parts for a group to read together. Scour your library's children's poetry collection for ideas. Consider using poems from Paul Flesichman's Newbery-winning *Joyful Noise: Poems for Two Voices*. Fleischman has several other books of poems for two voices, as well as *Big Talk: Poems for Four Voices*. They're great fun to read aloud.

Skits

If you have the space and the supplies, you can invite teens to create their own skits. Give them a place to start by giving them five or six props or costume pieces (two different hats, a stuffed toy, a cane, a lunchbox, and a scarf, for example) and a title ("First Day of School" or "Babysitting") and have them make up a skit to perform for the others.

You can also use some of the standard skit types from improvisational comedy. For example:

- *Questions only*. Give two teens a scene setting (school lunchroom, shopping mall, classroom, etc.). They are to have a conversation using only questions. If you want to involve more teens, you can rotate in a new player every time one person fails to respond in a question. See how long they can keep the scene going.
- *Alphabetical*. As discussed, give a scene setting. This time, also give a letter of the alphabet. The players must then have a conversation in which each sentence must begin with the subsequent letter of the alphabet. (So if the scene is the school lunchroom, and the start letter is D, the first person says, "Did you just get here?" Then the second one says, "Eating isn't my priority." Then the first one replies, "Funny that you feel that way," and the second responds, "Guess why?" and so on. As before, you can substitute waiting players in if a player fails to respond with the correct letter.
- *Song titles*. Same as "questions only," except the players must converse using only titles of songs.
- *Number of words*. In this one you can have four or even six players. Give them a scene to act out. Each player is given a number, and everything that player says must contain exactly that number of words.

MAKING AND CRAFTING

Craft and maker programs are often big hits with teens. You can set them up as drop-in programs or do them more formally. In a drop-in situation, you just need to have the materials and supplies laid out on a table or in your program area. You can either leave a sheet of instructions, or have someone stationed there to supervise and explain. If the craft involves more dangerous elements like sharp knives or hot glue guns, you will need to have an adult or older teen supervising.

Frankentoys

Frankentoys are created by taking apart old dolls and toys and reassembling the parts in random and unique ways—a stuffed dog with the head of a Barbie doll and legs made out of GI Joes, for example. Frankentoys are a big hit with teens, but doing a Frankentoys program does involve quite a bit of preparation. First, you need to collect old dolls, action figures, and toys from your library staff, friends, and the teens themselves. The more toys the better! Then you need to collect the materials you will need to take the toys apart and to put them back together. Demolition tools might include scissors, knives, razor blades, hacksaws, and hammers. Attachment tools might include various types of glue, including hot glue, duct tape, staples, and needles and thread. It's a good idea to have stations for the various activities—all the cutting tools in their own separate places, for example, and the reattachment tools in their own places. You will also need room for the teens to spread out the toys as they look for the pieces they want, and a place for them to put the discarded parts. If you have room, it would be great to display the creative results somewhere in the library.

Marshmallows and Spaghetti

A simple program you can do with inexpensive materials is building with only marshmallows (either mini-marshmallows, regular-sized, or a combination) and spaghetti. (Do be aware that a certain percentage of the marshmallows will get eaten!) For this program, you just need space to spread out the materials and allow everyone to be around a table. Stuff will get all over the floor, too, so you might want to consider what your floor surface is before taking this on. You can make this into a challenge: who can build the tallest tower, or who can build the tallest tower that will be strong enough to hold a book? Or you can just let their imaginations run wild. A colleague told me that when she did this program, a group of teen boys built a catapult and then used it to catapult marshmallows at a target they had drawn on a white board. You can also make it into a team-building exercise. Divide the teens into groups of three or four and give each group the same number of spaghetti sticks and marshmallows. Then give them a time limit (10 or 20 minutes) to see who can come up with the tallest or the strongest tower.

Painted Message Rocks

With a few simple supplies, your teens can paint on smooth river rocks, for use either as paper weights or as messages of kindness or support for others. You can buy river rocks at your local home improvement store. Get rocks that are 2–3 inches across. You can either leave them their natural color, or paint them black and allow them to dry. Then provide multiple colors of craft paint, oil-based paint pens, and thin paint brushes. The teens can then put designs on their rocks, or write in a positive message.

Check Teen Librarian Toolbox (http://www.teenlibrariantoolbox.com/tpib-programs/) or Teen Programming in Libraries on Pinterest (https://www.pinterest.com/heather_booth/teen-programming-in-libraries-a-collaborative-boar/) for dozens, if not hundreds, of ideas for crafts and making.

GAMES

For a holiday party or end of summer reading event, you may want to include some games. Here are a few that are always fun.

Icebreakers

Icebreaker activities with teens can be a challenge, because you want them to get to know one another, but you don't want to embarrass them or force them to reveal more about themselves than they are comfortable with. But if the teens don't know one another yet, icebreakers can be a fun way to help them talk to one another and learn something about one another.

You can ask them to line themselves up in different ways, for example:

- In alphabetical order by first name
- In alphabetical order by last name
- In order of your birthday, from January to December
- In order of how many languages you speak
- In order of how many places you have lived in
- In order of how many siblings you have

Another icebreaker is called "This or that?" Teens have to commit to one item or another, dividing themselves into two groups, one on each side of the room, based on their answers to the questions. Once they have divided themselves, ask another question so everyone has to shuffle around.

- Dogs or cats?
- Beach or mountains?
- Watch sports or play sports?
- Sweet or salty snacks?
- Country or city?
- Visit Europe or visit Asia?
- iOS or Android?
- Football or baseball?
- Hamburger or taco?
- Big party or small gathering?
- Sneakers or sandals?
- Cake or pie?
- Book or eBook?
- Ninjas or pirates?
- Dragons or unicorns?
- Marvel or DC?
- Blue or green?
- Apples or bananas?

This one gets them moving around and also lets them get to know one another.

Candy Ball

For this one, you can either prepare the ball yourself, or make it a separate project for the teens. You need about 50 or 60 pieces of wrapped candy; they can range from small pieces like Jolly Ranchers to regular-sized candy bars. On the whole, though, smaller size pieces are better. Start with a large candy bar or, for fun, a jingle bell as the center. Wrap it in bubble wrap to give the center some bulk, and tape it together. Then start wrapping it in a ball, using shrink wrap (use the sturdy wrap that movers use; kitchen plastic wrap is too thin and tears too easily. Place a piece of candy against the forming ball and continue to wrap. Repeat this process until you have used all your candy and the ball is as big as you want—the size of a basketball or even a beach ball, if you have a lot of teens. If you want to make the game a little more challenging, you can tape up the layers every so often.

To play the game, have the teens get in a circle. Hand the ball to one person and give two dice to the person on their left. The first player starts removing the layers, while the second person rolls the dice rapidly in an attempt to roll doubles. The first player gets to keep any candy he or she comes across, but must hand the ball to the person on the left as soon as that person rolls doubles. Then the play moves around the circle to the left. To add a level of complexity, you can have the players wear gloves as they unwrap the ball.

Giant Jenga

You can make your own set of giant-sized Jenga blocks using soft drink cartons. Jenga is the game in which you start with a sturdy tower of blocks, then each player in turn removes a block and places it on top of the tower, all without toppling the tower. Create your giant Jenga set by taking the boxes from 12-can cartons of sodas. Tape up the sides. If you really want to get fancy, you can cover them with wrapping paper or shelf paper. Have your teens work in teams, or have a tournament to see who can go the longest without toppling the tower.

Sticky Notes

Divide the teens into groups of four to six. Each group picks one person to be "it." Every other person in the group is given a package of sticky notes (like Post-It brand notes). Set a timer for five minutes or start playing a song. The teens with the sticky notes start sticking the notes onto their "it" person, with the goal to cover the person as completely as possible with the sticky notes before the timer goes off or the song ends. At this point, you can have the teens judge which "it" is the most thoroughly covered in sticky notes. Then, instruct the "it" people that when the next song starts playing, they have until the end of the song to get as many of the sticky notes as possible off their body—without using their hands.

FOOD

Having food for the participants at teen programs is a given, but you can also use food as a program. Decorating cookies or cupcakes is always fun. You can buy or make plain sugar cookies or plain cupcakes and provide a variety of items for them to use in decorating: icing, of course, but also candies, fruit, and even unusual things like bacon bits or dry cereal pieces. Either just turn the teens loose to decorate and eat their own or make it into a competition. You can do a "Cupcake Wars" type competition by giving each teen some icing and five items (e.g., red hots, M&Ms, raisins, Cheerios, and chocolate chips) and see who comes up with the most creative use of the items. Alternatively, you could provide a full range of items and ask each teen to decorate a cupcake that represents some aspect of a favorite book. The other teens could all judge the entries.

LIFE SKILLS

Having life skills programs for teens is a growing trend and easy to do with not a lot of space or equipment. Call your program "Adulting 101" or "How to Survive Adulthood." This program lends itself to a series, and it is one you can call on community members or colleagues to help you with. Here are some ideas for program sessions:

- *Financial health.* Invite a banker or financial manager to talk to the teens about topics like the difference between debit and credit cards, how to avoid scams, how to make a budget and save money, and how to get a good credit rating. Include a segment on how to keep your financial information safe and secure, especially when using online banking, and other smartphone financial apps.
- *Etiquette.* Dining dos and don'ts, how to meet new people, how to be courteous in any situation, writing thank-you notes, small talk, being a good guest.
- *Taking care of your body.* Invite a nutritionist and a fitness expert to talk about best practices for a healthy body. They can debunk common myths and share the latest research on what makes a good diet and what makes a good lifelong exercise routine. Include something on first aid—cleaning and dressing a wound, removing a splinter, what to do if someone is choking, and so forth.
- *Looking your best.* Bring in experts on grooming and make-up, or make this session more general by focusing on clothes: how to tell whether your clothes are good quality, and how to keep your clothes looking their best. Ask a few expert tailors or seamstresses to come in and show the teens how to take up a hem, patch a hole, or let out a seam. Encourage boys to come, too—I know a young man who made extra money in the service by doing mending for his fellow Marines.
- *Workplace know-how.* Invite supervisors and managers from your community (and library) to be on a panel where they share what they wish every employee knew. They can cover topics from applying for the job to how to dress and act at work to the importance of showing up on time.
- *Living on your own.* Cover topics that teens need to know about living on their own: how to find and rent an apartment, how to do laundry, how to do minor household repairs, how to know when to call the landlord (or the plumber) and what you can do yourself.
- *Car basics.* Start with how to buy a car, how to negotiate a price, how to get a car loan, and the basics of car insurance. Then move on to basic car maintenance, including checking oil and other fluids, checking tire pressure, changing a tire, and replacing windshield wipers. Include a segment on what to do if you get into a wreck.
- *Personal safety.* Invite a police officer or other safety professional to talk with teens about what they should know about keeping safe. Topics could include keeping safe at home, when traveling, at college, in the workplace, online, and more.

- *Careers.* This topic could itself be a series of programs. Invite local adults in to talk about their careers—how they got started, what they needed to study in school, what they wish they had known earlier. This can range from the trades (plumbers, builders, etc.) to the professions (medicine, law, etc.) and everything else. If you have local sports teams (major or minor league) find out if they can send a player or coach to talk to the teens about how they got where they are, and the importance of staying in school. Most teams have some sort of community outreach office. For other professions, if you don't know someone, try contacting a professional association for suggestions.

CONCLUSION

These are just a few suggestions for programs, but they are all programs that I have done or have seen work successfully. As I said in Chapter 4, the key for teen programs is not just finding out what the teens themselves want but getting them involved in designing, creating, and presenting programs. As Jennifer Velásquez said in a *School Library Journal* article (2014):

If three kids sit down and begin to play Magik, Risk, or something else, ask them if they'd like to lead a group activity in that game. When you spot someone playing chess, ask if she'd run a chess night. If a teen shows you his drawings, ask him if he will run an art evening. Offer to get the supplies if he will make a flier and arrange for some of his friends to come. Display the art to help mark teen territory.

Keep your eyes and ears open, and programs will suggest themselves to you.

REFERENCE

Velásquez, Jennifer. October 15, 2014. "The Trouble with Teen Programming." *School Library Journal.* Available at: http://www.slj.com/2014/10/teens-ya/the-trouble-with-teen-programming/.

APPENDIX C

Displays and Booklists

As discussed in Chapter 3, displays and booklists are good ways to do "stealth" or "passive" readers' advisory. An eye-catching display can introduce teens to books they never would have found on their own. Booklists can give teens a place to start looking for books that are similar to ones they like. What's more, booklists can help the library worker remember titles that might appeal. This appendix includes a number of booklists, as well as suggestions for how to utilize those titles in displays. Booklists can be printed on bookmark-sized cards, stored in a binder, or posted on the library's website.

BLIND DATE WITH A BOOK

There are many ways to do a "Blind Date with a Book" display. These are popular in libraries around Valentine's Day, but really you can do one any time. The idea is to cover the book in brown paper and write some hints about the book's contents on the cover. It's easiest to do this kind of display if your library uses RFID chips, because then you can simply wrap the entire book and it can still be checked out. If you use barcodes, you may have to make a cut-out to reveal the barcode.

If you're doing this for Valentine's Day, you might write the hints on paper hearts and attach them to the books. Otherwise, just write them directly on the front of the paper-covered book. Keep a list of what you have used, however, so you can rewrap the books and put them out when they come back!

You can write the hints in any way that works for you. Following are some examples of different kinds of blurbs.

This first set are written like personal ads, using the book's genre or type as the personality type, then giving a hint of the book's contents in the remaining words. Obviously, you would not include the author and title on the blurb. Some of these came from Molly Wetta's blog, Wrapped Up in Books (https://wrappedupinbooks.org).

Heartfelt and compelling contemporary story seeks reader who is not afraid to get in touch with her emotions. (*If I Stay*, Gayle Forman. Dutton, 2009.)

Award-winning book seeks adventurous reader not afraid of ghosts. (*Graveyard Book*, Neil Gaiman. HarperCollins, 2008.)

Fast-paced, heartfelt contemporary novel seeks sports fan. (*Boy 21*, Matthew Quick. Little Brown, 2012.)

Funny and sweet romance seeks a reader who is not afraid to take a dare. (*The Fine Art of Truth or Dare*, Melissa Jensen. Speak, 2012.)

Horror story seeks reader for the ultimate game of survival—the zombie apocalypse. (*The End Games*, by T. Michael Martin. HarperCollins, 2013.)

Tender romance where opposites attract seeks reader willing to look at both sides of a story. (*The Difference between You and Me*, Madeleine George. Viking, 2012.)

Epic fantasy seeks reader for a perilous journey to find kidnapped gods. (*Vessel*, Sarah Beth Durst. Margaret K. McElderry, 2012.)

Alternate history + urban fantasy hybrid seeks reader who isn't afraid of shadows. (*Shadow Society*, Marie Rutowski. Farrar, Straus and Giroux, 2012.)

Noir mystery seeks reader interested in unraveling a web of lies. (*White Cat*, Holly Black. Margaret K. McElderry, 2010.)

World War II novel seeks reader who believes that female friendships can defeat the Nazis. (*Code Name Verity*, Elizabeth Wein. Egmont, 2012.)

Quirky fantasy seeks reader who is willing to communicate with another world and help a boy find his father. (*Corner of White*, Jaclyn Moriarty. Arthur A. Levine, 2013.)

Funny paranormal seeks reader who enjoys boarding school hi-jinks. (*Hex Hall*, Rachel Hawkins. Hyperion, 2010.)

Quirky, award-winning road trip book seeks reader who will appreciate its dark sense of humor (must not be afraid of yard gnomes). (*Going Bovine*, Libba Bray. Delacorte, 2009.)

Gritty, inspiring realistic enjoys heartfelt stories of friendship under fire. (*Mexican Whiteboy*, Matt de la Peña. Delacorte, 2008.)

Smart and sophisticated book with a rebel heart seeks art appreciator willing to fall in love in just one night. (*Graffiti Moon*, Cath Crowley. Knopf, 2012.)

Charming romance seeks reader for a rendezvous in Paris. (*Anna and the French Kiss*, Stephanie Perkins. Dutton, 2010.)

Fairy tale retelling seeks reader to explore a curse on a family's woolen mill. (*Curse Dark as Gold*, Elizabeth Bunce. Arthur A. Levine, 2008.)

Fast-paced adventure story set in Australia seeks readers willing to fight for their country. (*Tomorrow, When the War Began*, John Marsden. Walker, 1995.)

This next set of blurbs just use a few key words about each book, including the setting, the style or genre, and something about the characters:

Teenage hackers, San Francisco, Homeland Security, adventure, suspense. (*Little Brother*, Cory Doctorow. Tor, 2008.)

Alternate version of Chicago, adventure, a "day" boy and a "night" girl, romance, government control. (*Plus One*, Elizabeth Fama. Farrar, Straus and Giroux, 2014.)

Australian slacker with dog, urban, mysterious mission, touching stories. (*I Am the Messenger*, Markus Zusak. Knopf, 2002.)

Teenage dad, graffiti artist, doomed love, tearjerker. (*The First Part Last*, by Angela Johnson. Simon & Schuster, 2003.)

True adventure and mystery, royalty, war, murder, class struggle. (*The Family Romanov*, Candice Fleming. Schwartz & Wade, 2014.)

Bicycles, beaches, divorced parents, romance, self-discovery. (*Along for the Ride*, Sarah Dessen. Viking, 2009.)

Plymouth Massachusetts, mermaids, magic, myth, history, curses, murder. (*Monstrous Beauty*, Elizabeth Fama. Farrar, Straus and Giroux, 2012.)

Science fiction, space, aliens, deceit, revenge. (*Tin Star*, Cecil Castellucci. Roaring Brook, 2008.)

The Mooresville Public Library's Savvy Reader blog (http://mpl-yaz.blogspot.com) uses a format that's more like a movie trailer. They start with a tagline, then follow it up with some hints about the book's content. Here are some examples in that style:

Everything I learned, I learned from the movies. I'm an amateur filmmaker who hopes to make a difference in the lives of others. I'm looking for someone who will support my efforts and isn't afraid of a good cry. Will you buy my ticket? (*Me and Earl and the Dying Girl*, Jesse Andrews. Amulet Books, 2012.)

Eat your heart out. Life is waging war everyday just to survive, but it's a lot easier with someone by your side. I'm looking for a trace of humanity in this world—do you have the heart to stick with me? (*Ashes*, Ilsa Bick. Egmont, 2011.)

More than a pretty face. I used to think that looks were the most important thing, until a plane crash changed my pageant plans. Now I'm a warrior who can wrestle snakes and survive in the wild. Will you take me *au naturel*? (*Beauty Queens*, Libba Bray. Scholastic, 2011.)

You've stolen my heart. I used to lead a life of crime, but I got out of the game. But you dragged me back in when you stole my heart. Will you be my partner in crime? (*Heist Society*, Ally Carter. Hyperion, 2010.)

It's like déjà vu all over again. I'm an American Girl in London, looking for an adventure. But the new attacks *ripped* from old headlines have left me reeling. Can you help me figure out what's going on? (*Name of the Star*, Maureen Johnson. Putnam, 2011.)

Can't watch Dexter? Then check me out. Being raised in the family business has left its mark on me, but it turns out that I have a rare insight into the investigation of a new serial killer. Can we solve the crime together? (*I Hunt Killers*, Barry Lyga. Little Brown, 2012.)

There's no place like home. I'm looking to reclaim the land and break the curse, but I can't do it alone. Will you come with me on this quest? (*Finnikin of the Rock*, Melina Marchetta. Candlewick, 2010.)

I can see another world in your eyes. Unfortunately, it's a dark and dangerous world. I'm starting to wonder if I'm losing my mind. Can you help me see things clearly? (*Marbury Lens*, Andrew Smith. Feiwel and Friends, 2010.)

What are the chances of love at first sight? What are the chances you'll fall in love within 24 hours? What are the chances you can find someone again once you've lost them? Will you help me do the math? (*Statistical Probability of Love at First Sight*, Jennifer E. Smith. Little Brown, 2012.)

Sticks and stones . . . Words really can hurt. Reputations can change by the casual words of a stranger. So what do you have to say? (*The List*, Siobhan Vivian. Scholastic Push, 2012.)

GENTLE CHICK LIT

These are titles that are basically light romances, with no explicit sex. They all deal with other issues (family, friendship, etc.) as well. For a display, consider using pink signage, hearts, flowers. Possible props could include feathers, butterflies, sparkles, high heels.

Asher, Jay. *What Light*. Razorbill, 2016. Sierra spends every Christmas season with her family selling Christmas trees in California. However, in what might be her last Christmas in California, Sierra decides to make it memorable.

Buxbaum, Julie. *Tell Me Three Things*. Delacorte, 2016. Still reeling from the death of her mother, Jessie finds herself adrift with a new stepfamily, a new school, and a new e-mail pen pal called somebody/nobody. Can Jessie rely on somebody/nobody?

Czukas, Liz. *Top Ten Clues You're Clueless*. HarperTeen, 2014. Chloe, an avid list-making diabetic, is stuck in the breakroom at work on Christmas Eve because her store manager is accusing her of stealing from charity. Can Chloe clear her name and learn a lesson about people along the way?

Dessen, Sarah. *Along for the Ride*. Viking, 2009. Spending the summer in a beach town with her dad and his new wife and baby gives Auden a chance to explore some of the things she has missed out on in her oh-so-responsible life so far.

Forman, Gayle. *Just One Day*. Speak, 2013. Allyson's entire life is meticulously planned by her mother, yet on a guided tour of Europe, Allyson decides that she needs just one day that is of her own invention.

Han, Jenny. *To All the Boys I've Loved Before*. Simon & Schuster, 2014. Ever write a letter to someone you know will never receive it? Ever have that letter delivered by accident? Lara Jean did and now there are consequences.

Leder, Meg. *The Museum of Heartbreak*. Simon Pulse, 2016. Everyone develops their own way of coping with heartbreak. For Penelope, curating a museum of items that signify her life might just do the trick.

Matson, Morgan. *Amy and Roger's Epic Detour*. Simon & Schuster, 2010. Amy's mom has arranged for Roger to drive Amy across the country. Amy's mom has set the route, planned the stops, and booked the hotels. But both Amy and Roger have their own goals and plans for this trip.

Oliver, Lauren. *Before I Fall*. HarperCollins, 2010. What would you do if you knew this was your last day? Samantha is about to find out as she discovers that she is reliving her last day over and over again.

Perkins, Stephanie. *Anna and the French Kiss*. Dutton, 2010. Moving schools in your senior year is not ideal. But for Anna, that new school is a boarding school in Paris, France. What could go wrong?

Sales, Leila. *This Song Will Save Your Life*. Farrar, Straus and Giroux, 2013. Elise discovers her passion and talent as a disc jockey.

Smith, Jennifer E. *The Statistical Probability of Love at First Sight*. Little Brown, 2012. Hadley would like to be anywhere but on a plane to England to attend her father's second marriage to a woman she's never met. But then she meets Oliver.

Smith, Jennifer E. *This Is What Happy Looks Like*. Headline, 2013. Can a relationship that started online go offline? Graham and Ellie are about to find out.

Welch, Jenna Evans. *Love and Gelato*. Simon Pulse, 2016. Lina is spending the summer in Tuscany, where she is given a journal that her late mother kept years ago. What will she learn about her mother, her father, and herself?

West, Kasie. *The Fill-In Boyfriend*. HarperTeen, 2015. What is a girl to do when her boyfriend dumps her at the door before prom? Find a replacement and convince everyone in the school that he is your boyfriend, of course.

TWICE UPON A TIME: FAIRY TALES RETOLD

For a display, decorate with anything that reminds you of fairy tales: pictures of castles, crowns, princes and princesses, a frog, a horse, an ogre, gold, and sparkles.

Block, Francesca Lia. *The Rose and the Beast: Fairy Tales Retold*. HarperCollins, 2001. Lyrical and modern retellings of beloved fairy tales such as *Snow White*, *Thumbelina*, *Cinderella*, and many others.

Bunce, Elizabeth C. *A Curse Dark as Gold*. Arthur A. Levine, 2008. In this retelling of Rumpelstiltkin, 17-year-old Charlotte struggles to keep the family's woolen mill running in the face of an overwhelming mortgage. When a man who can spin straw into gold shows up, she must decide if his help is worth the price.

Cross, Sarah. *Kill Me Softly*. Egmont, 2012. Mira's godmothers have ensured that Mira has lived a happy but protected life, but when she goes to her birthplace she finds that everyone is living a fairytale life—including Mira.

Dixon, Heather. *Entwined*. Greenwillow, 2011. In this retelling of the *Twelve Dancing Princesses*, Azalea and her 11 younger sisters have been forbidden to dance since their mother's death, but Azalea has discovered a hidden path in their castle where they can dance their sorrow away.

Durst, Sarah Beth. *Ice*. Margaret K. McElderry, 2009. Cassie embarks on a journey through unbelievable wonders and countless dangers that will bring her east of the sun and west of the moon as she chases her truest desires for her future.

Flinn, Alex. *Beastly*. HarperTeen, 2007. In this version of *Beauty and the Beast*, Kyle Kingsbury is rich, popular, handsome, and really spoiled. But when Kyle crosses the wrong girl, he discovers that he now looks as ugly as he acts.

Gaiman, Neil. *The Sleeper and the Spindle*. Bloomsbury, 2014. A dark combination retelling of *Snow White* and *Sleeping Beauty*, illustrated by Chris Riddell.

George, Jessica Day. *Princess of the Midnight Ball*. Bloomsbury, 2009. In this retelling of the *Twelve Dancing Princesses*, an ex-soldier named Galen discovers the secret that causes the sisters to dance every night and releases them from the enchantment, with the help of knitting.

Gruber, Michael. *The Witch's Boy*. HarperCollins, 2005. A unique take on Rumpelstiltskin that also incorporates other tales, including *Cinderella, Hansel & Gretel, Jack and the Beanstalk*, and more.

Haddix, Margaret Peterson. *Just Ella*. Simon & Schuster, 1999. In this continuation of the story of *Cinderella*, things don't necessarily end with happily ever after, as Ella finds that her happiness may not lie inside the castle with the prince.

Hodge, Rosamund. *Cruel Beauty*. Balzer & Bray, 2014. Nyx arrives at the castle of Ignifex, prepared to seduce him, marry him, and then kill him, breaking a long curse. But she discovers that there is more to Ignifex than she ever could have imagined. Retelling of *Beauty and the Beast*.

Kontis, Alethea. *Enchanted*. Houghton Mifflin Harcourt, 2012. In this retelling of the *Frog Prince*, Sunday Woodcutter makes friends with a frog, and then later with a prince, not realizing they are the one and the same.

Lanagan, Margo. *Tender Morsels*. Knopf, 2008. Liga, a young woman who endured unspeakable anguish, is magically whisked away to a fantasy realm to raise her daughters in peace. But as her daughters grow, the cracks between their fantasy life and the real world begin to show and all three women must make a choice about what world they want to live in. Retelling of *Snow White* and *Rose Red*.

Lewis, R. C. *Stitching Snow*. Disney Press, 2014. In this retelling of *Snow White*, Essie lives in subzero temperatures on the planet Thanda, tinkering with her seven mining drones, but when a mysterious stranger named Dane literally crashes in her life, a secret is revealed.

Lin, Grace. *Where the Mountain Meets the Moon*. Little Brown, 2009. Seeking to change her family's increasingly bad fortune, Minli sets out on a quest to find the mythical Old Man of the Moon. Soon, Minli's quest becomes intertwined with a series of ancient Chinese fairy tales.

Marillier, Juliet. *Wildwood Dancing*. Knopf, 2007. At the full moon, Jena and her sisters travel through a portal in the Transylvanian woods near their home to go dancing in the mysterious Wildwood with creatures rarely seen outside of fairy tales. When their father falls ill, Jena must figure out how to save her family.

McKinley, Robin. *Beauty: A Retelling of the Story Beauty and the Beast*. HarperCollins, 1978. Beauty has never felt like her nickname fits her—after all, she isn't beautiful—but when her father promises her to the Beast, she is determined to be courageous.

Meyer, Marissa. *Cinder*. Feiwel and Friends, 2012. This version of the Cinderella story is set in New Beijing—a city facing plague and intergalactic takeover. Cinder is a cyborg mechanic who forms an unlikely friendship with Prince Kai.

Pearce, Jackson. *Sisters Red*. Little Brown, 2010. A dark and sometimes violent retelling of *Little Red Riding Hood*, this book features the sisters Scarlett and Rosie, armed with bright red cloaks and sharp weapons, who fight against the Fenris—werewolves—who hunt and kill young girls.

Schmidt, Gary D. *Straw into Gold*. Houghton Mifflin Harcourt, 2009. Tousle and Innes are ordered by the king to solve a riddle, so they begin a harrowing journey to meet up with the queen to get their answer. The book explores the question of what might have happened if the queen in the Rumpelstiltskin story had not been able to guess his name.

Sheehan, Anna. *A Long, Long Sleep.* Gollancz, 2011. In this sci-fi take on *Sleeping Beauty*, Rosalinda has been asleep for 62 years—sleeping straight through dark times that killed millions and utterly changed the world. Hailed upon her awakening as the long-lost heir to an interplanetary empire, she is thrust alone into a dangerous future.

Yolen, Jane. *Briar Rose.* Random House, 1988. Rebecca's dying grandmother, Gemma, tells her, "I am Briar Rose." Rebecca knows that Gemma's version of the *Sleeping Beauty* story is a little different from the traditional one, but her quest to find out what Gemma means leads her directly into the Holocaust and her own family's history.

ROYAL READS

For a display, consider a background of crowns, thrones, scepters, castles, and so on.

Aveyard, Victoria. *Red Queen.* HarperTeen, 2015. Society is divided into reds and silvers. Mare, a 17-year-old girl, is part of the lower class known as the reds. When she is working at a royal event, her world is turned upside down when her powers are revealed.

Blake, Kendare. *Three Dark Crowns.* HarperTeen, 2016. On the night of their 16th birthday, three sisters who are heir to the throne must fight to the death to win the title of queen. Each girl has a set of powers she claims to possess.

Cabot, Meg. *The Princess Diaries.* HarperTeen, 2000. New York City girl Mia is heir to the throne of Genovia.

Carson, Rae. *The Girl of Fire and Thorns.* Greenwillow, 2011. Princess Elisa is an overweight, insecure 16-year-old who has been married off to a king. On her way to meet him, she is kidnapped. As she fights to survive, she loses her insecurities and embraces her destiny.

Cass, Kiera. *The Selection.* HarperTeen, 2012. In a world where a caste system determines so much of life, a contest is announced that will select 35 girls to compete for a chance at Prince Maxon's hand in marriage. America thought she would be the last person in the world to ever be selected.

Chima, Cinda Williams. *The Demon King.* Hyperion, 2009. Han, a former street thief, and Princess Raisa, an unlikely pair, join forces to uncover a conspiracy in the Wolf court.

Fine, Sarah. *The Impostor Queen.* Margaret K. McElderry, 2016. Elli was chosen to succeed the queen but upon the queen's death Elli does not, as expected, inherit the magic of ice and fire. Instead Elli must find her way in the world and deal with what that means for the kingdom.

George, Jessica Day. *Princess of the Midnight Ball.* Bloomsbury USA, 2009. In this retelling of the *Twelve Dancing Princesses*, an ex-soldier named Galen discovers the secret that causes the sisters to dance every night and releases them from the enchantment, with the help of knitting.

Hale, Shannon. *Princess Academy.* Bloomsbury USA, 2005. The next princess will be found in a particular town; unfortunately, none of the girls there are educated, let alone suitably well-mannered for court. So the girls are rounded up and sent to board in a nearby castle, where they learn reading, needlework, and commerce.

Kagawa, Julie. *The Iron King*. Harlequin Teen, 2010. On Meghan's 16th birthday, her little brother is kidnapped and she must travel into the fairy world to get him back. It is there she learns she is a princess and has power she never dreamed of.

Maas, Sarah J. *Throne of Glass*. Bloomsbury USA, 2012. Caleana, an 18-year-old assassin, is given an opportunity by Crown Prince Dorian to compete against 23 other men in exchange for a chance to serve 4 years as his assassin and then be granted freedom.

Meadows, Jodi. *The Orphan Queen*. Katherine Tegan, 2015. Princess Wilhelmina must fight to get her throne back after her parents were killed 10 years ago. She and her best friend pose as nobles and infiltrate the kingdom on their path to revolution.

Meyer, Marissa. *Cinder*. Feiwel and Friends, 2012. Cinder is a cyborg mechanic whose life suddenly becomes involved with that of Prince Kai and with the Lunar Queen.

Nix, Garth. *A Confusion of Princes*. Allen & Unwin, 2012. Taken from his parents as a child and equipped with biological and technological improvements, Khemri is now an enhanced human being, trained and prepared for the glory of becoming a prince of the empire. Only—oops!—turns out he's not the only one!

HUNGRY FOR A GOOD BOOK?

Consider a background with pictures of food (cupcakes, pizza, burgers, etc.). Use baking implements (cupcake pans, spatulas, mixing bowls, etc.) in your display.

Anderson, M. T. *Burger Wuss*. Candlewick, 1999. Hoping to lose his loser image, Anthony plans revenge on a bully, which results in a war between two competing fast-food restaurants.

Bauer, Joan. *Hope Was Here*. Putnam, 2000. Hope and her aunt move to small-town Wisconsin to take over the local diner.

Caletti, Deb. *Fortunes of Indigo Skye*. Simon & Schuster, 2008. Indigo is perfectly happy as a waitress at a local café—but when a mysterious stranger leaves her a $2.5 million tip, life is definitely going to change.

Davis, Tanita S. *A La Carte*. Knopf, 2008. Lainey dreams of becoming the first African American female chef to have her own vegetarian cooking show. But the return of an old friend disrupts her life and her relationships.

Dessen, Sarah. *The Truth about Forever*. Penguin, 2004. Macy finds that working for a catering company exposes you to life's celebrations and its catastrophes.

Dessen, Sarah. *Keeping the Moon*. Viking, 1999. When Colie is sent to live with her aunt in a beach town in North Carolina, she doesn't realize that she'll end up working at the Last Chance Café, where she'll learn quite a bit about friendship, self-confidence, and beauty.

Fergus, Maureen. *Recipe for Disaster*. Kids Can Press, 2009. Francie has a part-time baking business and dreams of the day that she'll have her own TV cooking show. Everything seems to be going along perfectly until a new girl shows up at school.

Hepler, Heather. *The Cupcake Queen*. Dutton, 2009. Penny Lane feels out of place since she has moved to middle of nowhere. Her mother has opened up a cupcake shop and Penny's parents are taking a "break". Penny just wants things to get back to how they used to be but she finds out quickly that things don't always work out how you want them to.

Nelson, Suzanne. *Cake Pop Crush*. Scholastic, 2013. Ali loves to bake, which is good, since she helps her dad in his bakery. She agrees to compete in a bake-off, and it turns out her competition includes the cute son of the owner of the rival coffee/pastry shop across the street.

Ockler, Sarah. *Bittersweet*. Simon Pulse, 2012. Love, ice skating, family, hope, dreams, trying, wanting, and lots and lots of cupcakes (Vanilla cupcakes topped with whipped peanut butter cream cheese icing, milk chocolate chips, crushed pretzels, and a drizzle of warm caramel, anyone?)

Ostow, Micol. *Crush du Jour*. Simon Pulse, 2007. Teaching a cooking class, working at a restaurant, studying for her SATs—Laine has a busy life! What she doesn't need is a rival for the affections of her crush.

Shaw, Tucker. *Flavor of the Week*. Disney-Hyperion, 2003. Overweight high school senior Cyril has two loves: cooking and Rose. Of the two, he considers cooking the only attainable goal.

Weeks, Sarah. *Pie*. Scholastic, 2011. Aunt Polly died and left her secret pie recipe to her cat Lardo, and left Lardo to Alice. Now Alice finds out that people want that pie recipe so bad, and they will go through almost anything to get it.

Whytock, Cherry. *My Cup Runneth Over: The Life of Angelica Cookson Potts*. Simon Pulse, 2003. Angelica loves food—cooking it and eating it. But when your mother is a former fashion model, the subject of food can be a difficult one.

FROM THE MALE POINT OF VIEW

Use a background with pictures of boys/young men, sports equipment, bicycles, motorcycles, shoes/boots, and so on.

Anderson, Laurie Halse. *Twisted*. Viking, 2007. A prank followed by court-ordered service turn Tyler from a nerdy junior into a hot senior. But do his insides match his outside?

Beaudoin, Sean. *Wise Young Fool*. Little, Brown, 2013. While Richie Sudden is stuck in juvie, he has time to ponder his life and what got him here.

Green, John. *An Abundance of Katherines*. Dutton, 2006. Colin has had exactly 19 girlfriends, all of whom have dumped him, and all of whom were named Katherine. Solution: road trip!

Horowitz, Anthony. *Stormbreaker*. Penguin, 2001. Alex Rider is recruited by MI-6 to be a spy after the death of his uncle.

Jenkins, A. M. *Damage*. HarperCollins, 2001. Austin has it all—he's handsome, well-off, and a star football player. Then why doesn't he want to live?

Jenkins, A. M. *Repossessed*. HarperCollins, 2007. Kiriel is bored with being a demon. So he decides to try physical existence for a while and inhabits the body of a teenager.

Johnson, Angela. *The First Part Last*. Simon & Schuster, 2003. On Bobby's 16th birthday, his girlfriend Nia handed him a balloon and said, "Bobby, I've got something to tell you." Now Bobby is raising his daughter, Feather.

McBride, Lish. *Hold Me Closer, Necromancer*. Henry Holt, 2010. Turns out Seattle is full of werewolves, necromancers, and other not-quite-human people. Sam is a necromancer, and someone has sensed his latent powers and wants to eliminate him.

Scalzi, John. *Redshirts*. Tor, 2012. Ensign Andy Dahl and his friends on the Universal Union flagship *Intrepid* begin to notice that new crew members have a very high mortality rate.

Scieszcka, Jon. *Knucklehead*. Viking, 2008. When you grow up with five brothers, life is full of broken bones, comments about bodily functions, practical jokes, and more.

Smith, Andrew. *Winger*. Simon & Schuster, 2013. Ryan is a 14-year-old at a co-ed boarding school, dealing with his crush on his 16-year-old best friend Annie, his rugby teammates, and a jock who wants to kill him.

Zusak, Markus. *Getting the Girl*. Arthur A. Levine, 2003. It's probably not the greatest idea in the world to fall for your older brother's girlfriend, but that's what Cameron does.

BOARDING SCHOOL BOOKS

Use a background of old-fashioned buildings; dorm rooms.

Bradley, Alan. *As Chimney Sweepers Come to Dust*. Delacorte, 2015. Flavia de Luce is shipped across the ocean to boarding school in Toronto. When a body comes crashing down out of the chimney and into her room, Flavia starts investigating.

Bray, Libba. *A Great and Terrible Beauty*. Simon & Schuster, 2003. In the Victorian era, Gemma has grown up in India, but now she has been sent back to England to attend Spence. She brings with her a sense of foreboding that she cannot shake or seem to share with anyone.

Carriger, Gail. *Etiquette & Espionage*. Little, Brown, 2013. Mademoiselle Geraldine's Finishing Academy for Young Ladies of Quality teaches its girls how to dance, dress, and eat properly, of course. But it also teaches death, diversion, and espionage!

Cavallaro, Brittany. *A Study in Charlotte*. Katherine Tegen, 2016. Holmes (Charlotte) and Watson (Jamie) are students at Sherringford Prep, and they're both being framed for murder.

Carter, Allie. *I'd Tell You I Love You, But Then I'd Have to Kill You*. Hyperion, 2006. The Gallagher Academy for Exceptional Young Women is a school for very bright girls—who also want to be spies.

Green, John. *Looking for Alaska*. Dutton, 2005. Miles is looking for the Great Perhaps—and an Alabama boarding school offers the possibility of finding it, especially after he meets the captivating, unpredictable, and utterly alive Alaska.

Hale, Shannon. *Princess Academy*. Bloomsbury, 2005. The next princess will be found in a particular town; unfortunately, none of the girls there are educated, let alone suitably well-mannered for court. So the girls are rounded up and sent to board in a nearby castle, where they learn reading, needlework, and commerce.

Horowitz, Anthony. *Point Blank*. Penguin, 2001. Alex Rider goes undercover at a prep school.

Johnson, Maureen. *The Name of the Star*. Putnam, 2011. Rory's family has moved from Louisiana to England, so she is beginning her senior year at a boarding school in London—just in time for a new outbreak of Jack the Ripper-style murders.

Kuehn, Stephanie. *Charm & Strange*. St. Martin's, 2013. Win, who is now in boarding school in Vermont, was once a 10-year-old tennis phenom known as Drew. What happened?

Lockhart, E. *The Disreputable History of Frankie Landau-Banks*. Hyperion, 2008. When Frankie learns that her boyfriend is a member of an all-boy secret society at their boarding school, she decides to make a statement.

Marchetta, Melina. *Saving Francesca*. Knopf, 2006. Francesca is one of the "lucky" 30 girls in the first co-ed class at St. Sebastian's school.

Marchetta, Melina. *On the Jellicoe Road*. Harper, 2008. Taylor is elected as a leader in the territory war games played by her school with the Townies (locals) and Cadets. Taylor has very few memories of her childhood but certain events cause her to begin a relentless quest for answers.

Mead, Richelle. *Vampire Academy*. Razorbill, 2007. Lissa is a mortal vampire. Rose is her best friend and protector. They attend St. Vladimir's Academy, where there's a lot more going on than just classes and exams.

Perkins, Stephanie. *Anna and the French Kiss*. Dutton, 2010. Moving schools in your senior year is not ideal. But for Anna, that new school is a boarding school in Paris, France. What could go wrong?

Rowling, J.K. *Harry Potter and the Sorcerer's Stone*. Scholastic, 1998. When 11-year-old Harry learns that he is a wizard, he is able to escape from the drudgery of his life to the amazing Hogwarts School of Witchcraft and Wizardry.

Smith, Andrew. *Winger*. Simon & Schuster, 2013. Ryan is a 14-year-old at a co-ed boarding school, dealing with his crush on his 16-year-old best friend Annie, his rugby teammates, and a jock who wants to kill him.

Stiefvater, Maggie. *Raven Boys*. Scholastic, 2012. Blue has a policy of staying away from Aglionby school boys. Known as Raven Boys, they can only mean trouble. But then she meets Gansey, who is obsessed with the supernatural; Adam, who yearns for a life outside what he knows; Ronan, whose anger hides untold regret; and Noah, a troubled soul who knows more than he lets on.

Vanderpool, Claire. *Navigating Early*. Delacorte, 2013. Kansas boy Jack is sent to boarding school in rural Maine, where he meets Early Auden, who sees the number pi as a story and is on a quest to find a great black bear.

IT'S THE END OF THE WORLD AS WE KNOW IT: POST-APOCALYPTIC FICTION

For a display, use a stark, black/white/grey background. Decorate with flames and ashes. Or paint a skyline with destroyed buildings. Have pictures of broken-down automobiles or other technology.

Baciagalupi, Paolo. *Shipbreaker*. Little, Brown, 2010. The planet's natural resources are exhausted, global warming is happening, Antarctica is gone, cities drowned.

Nailer makes his living stripping metal from old ships, to be sold to for recycling. His life takes a turn when he comes across a wrecked ship whose only survivor is a girl who is the heir to one of the biggest corporations in the world.

Bick, Ilsa J. *Ashes*. Egmont, 2011. First, there's a cataclysmic electromagnetic pulse. Dead birds fall from the sky. Deer run off a cliff, maddened for unknown reasons. And people drop dead instantaneously and inexplicably—or they are miraculously, irrevocably changed, some for the better, and some for the worse.

Block, Francesca Lia. *Love in the Time of Global Warming*. Henry Holt, 2013. A retelling of the *Odyssey*, set after a Los Angeles earthquake.

Collins, Suzanne. *The Hunger Games*. Scholastic, 2008. After a great war, North America is now Panem, divided into 12 districts. Each year, each district must send one boy and one girl to the Hunger Games, to fight to the death.

Dick, Philip K. *Do Androids Dream of Electric Sheep?* Doubleday, 1968. Source of the movie *Blade Runner*. After war has killed millions, companies build androids to replace animals and even people. Rick Deckard is an officially sanctioned bounty hunter whose job is to find rogue androids and retire them.

King, Stephen. *The Stand*. Doubleday, 1978. After a virus kills 99 percent of the population, the survivors coalesce around two foci: the good in Boulder; the others following the evil Randall Flagg in Las Vegas.

Lloyd, Saci. *The Carbon Diaries 2015*. Holiday House, 2010. Laura chronicles the first year of mandatory British carbon rationing, after the world's resources are depleted.

Maberry, Jonathan. *Rot & Ruin*. Simon & Schuster, 2010. Fifteen years after the zombies took over the world, Benny lives in a small fenced-in community and prefers to stay there in safety. But now he's 15 and must work or lose half his rations.

Mandel, Emily St. John. *Station Eleven*. Knopf, 2014. After a deadly flu kills off most of the world, the survivors have to decide what it really means to be human.

McCarthy, Cormac. *The Road*. Knopf, 2006. A man and his young son are traveling along a highway, hoping to get far enough south to avoid the onslaught of winter. The land is cold, barren, ash-ridden and abandoned, and they have all their worldly goods in a wonky shopping cart.

Mullin, Mike. *Ashfall*. Tanglewood Press, 2011. When the super volcano underneath Yellowstone erupts, Alex's camping weekend suddenly becomes a nightmare. He must fight for his survival and find his family in a world of darkness, ash, and violence.

Nix, Garth. *Shade's Children*. HarperCollins, 1997. Four teenagers escape from evil overlords who rule a future where humans don't live past age 14, and all adults have disappeared.

O'Brien, Robert C. *Z for Zachariah*. Atheneum, 1975. Ann Burden lives alone in a protected valley after a nuclear war has destroyed everyone and everything else. But then a man walks into the valley, wearing a safe suit. Is he friend or foe?

Pfeffer, Susan Beth. *Life as We Knew It*. Houghton Mifflin Harcourt, 2006. When a meteor knocks the moon closer to Earth, Miranda and her family must learn how to survive.

Roth, Veronica. *Divergent*. Katherine Tegan, 2011. In a post-apocalyptic Chicago, people are divided into five factions. At 16, everyone is divided into his or her faction. But what if, like Tris, you don't quite fit: you're Divergent?

Stephenson, Neil. *Seveneves*. William Morrow, 2015. Five-thousand years after a disintegrating moon destroyed life on Earth, the seven different groups of survivors begin to return to the planet.

Walker, Karen Thompson. *Age of Miracles*. Random House, 2012. As the rotation of the Earth slows down, life continues for Julia as she navigates through the trials of middle school.

Wells, Dan. *Partials*. Balzer + Bray, 2012. In the year 2076, 11 years after an airborne viral outbreak, the average newborn lives just 56 hours. Sixteen-year-old Kira Walker, a young medic interning at a hospital, thinks that the key to human survival lies in studying Partials, a group of rogue cyborgs described as "unthinking, unfeeling human killers."

Yancey, Rick. *The 5th Wave*. Putnam, 2013. After surviving four waves of destruction, Cassie must trust a mysterious boy in order to rescue her brother and fight an invasion of murderous human look-alikes.

ROAD TRIPS

Use maps in background. Include pictures of roads, motels, roadside diners, receipts, and so forth.

Arnold, David. *Mosquitoland*. Viking, 2015. When she learns that her mother is sick in Ohio, Mim confronts her demons on a thousand-mile odyssey from Mississippi that redefines her notions of love, loyalty, and what it means to be sane.

Bray, Libba. *Going Bovine*. Delacorte, 2009. Cameron, a 16-year-old slacker, sets off on a madcap road trip along with a punk angel, a dwarf sidekick, a yard gnome and a mad scientist to save the world and perhaps his own life.

Doktorski, Jennifer. *How My Summer Went Up in Flames*. Simon Pulse, 2013. Placed under a temporary restraining order for torching her former boyfriend's car, 17-year-old Rosie embarks on a cross-country car trip from New Jersey to Arizona, while waiting for her court appearance.

Graham, Hilary Weisman. *Reunited*. Simon & Schuster, 2012. Alice, Summer, and Tiernan were best friends who broke up at the same time as their favorite band, but four years later, just before they are preparing to go off to college, the girls reluctantly come back together, each with her own motives, for a road trip from Massachusetts to Austin, Texas, for the band's one-time-only reunion concert.

Green, John. *An Abundance of Katherines*. Dutton, 2006. Colin has had exactly 19 girlfriends, all of whom have dumped him, and all of whom were named Katherine. Solution: road trip!

Johnson, Maureen. *13 Little Blue Envelopes*. HarperCollins, 2005. Ginny Blackstone is a reluctant adventurer as she follows her aunt Peg's mysterious instructions via 13 little blue letters in a surprise trip through Europe.

Kirby, Jessi. *In Honor*. Simon & Schuster, 2012. Three days after she learns that her brother Finn died serving in Iraq, Honor receives a letter from him asking her to drive his car from Texas to California for a concert, and when his estranged best friend shows up suddenly and offers to accompany her, they set off on a road trip that reveals much about all three of them.

Lacour, Nina. *The Disenchantments*. Dutton, 2012. A week-long road trip with the girl band he helped to found leads Colby from San Francisco to Portland, Oregon, and involves seedy motels, a dance party, hot tubs, an impulsive tattoo, graffiti, and very little sleep, as well as some insights into his life.

Mackler, Carolyn. *Guyaholic*. Candlewick, 2007. Ever since V's mom dumped her with her grandparents, she's bounced from guy to guy, until she meets Sam. But V at her graduation party does something that risks losing Sam forever, so she heads out to visit her mom in hopes of putting two thousand miles between herself, Sam, and the wreckage of that night.

Matson, Morgan. *Amy and Roger's Epic Detour*. Simon & Schuster, 2010. Amy's mom has arranged for Roger to drive Amy across the country. Amy's mom has set the route, planned the stops, and booked the hotels. But, both Amy and Roger have their own goals and plans for this trip.

Smith, Jennifer E. *You Are Here*. Simon & Schuster, 2009. Emma has never felt that she fit in with the rest of her family, so when she discovers that she had a twin brother who died shortly after they were born, she takes off on an impulsive road trip to try to discover who she really is.

IT'S ONLY ROCK & ROLL . . .

Include items such as concert tickets, guitars, drums, and CDs in your display or on a background.

Ahonen, J. P. *Sing No Evil*. Abrams, 2014. In this graphic novel, Aksel, a 20-something guitarist leader of a heavy metal band, happens to stutter when he sings. Life becomes messy and he finds himself in a battle to save his city from supernatural forces set loose by ancient music.

Benway, Robin. *Audrey, Wait!* Razorbill, 2008. "Audrey, Wait" is the hit new breakup song. Audrey is the real girl it was written about, and she's not thrilled about being famous for dumping a rock star.

Castellucci, Cecil. *Beige*. Candlewick, 2009. Dad's an aging L.A. punk rocker known as the Rat. Daughter's a buttoned-up neat freak who'd rather be anywhere else. Can this summer be saved?

Going, K. L. *Fat Kid Rules the World*. Penguin Putnam, 2003. Troy is obese and depressed. A homeless teenage punk-rock icon rescues Troy from a suicide attempt and convinces him to become a drummer for his new band.

Goode, Laura. *Sister Mischief*. Candlewick, 2011. A Jewish, lesbian, teenaged MC and her all-female rap collective take on their school when their principal bans hip-hop.

Kelly, Tara. *Amplified*. Henry Holt, 2011. When spoiled 17-year-old Jasmine Kiss gets kicked out of her house by her father, she flees to Santa Cruz, California, to pursue her dream of becoming a rock musician.

Kuehnert, Stephanie. *I Wanna Be Your Joey Ramone*. MTV Books, 2008. Emily Black's mother abandoned her when she was four months old, hitting the road to follow a punk band. Now Emily is all grown up and she has a punk band of her own.

Lacour, Nina. *The Disenchantments.* Dutton, 2012. The summer after high school, Colby goes on tour with the Disenchantments, and all-girl band he helped to found.

McCarry, Sarah. *All Our Pretty Songs.* St. Martin's, 2013. In the grunge-rock era in the Pacific Northwest, the bond between two best friends is challenged when a mysterious and gifted musician comes between them and awakens an ancient evil.

McNally, Janet. *Girls in the Moon.* HarperTeen, 2016. Phoebe and Luna are the daughters of Meg and Kieran, former members of the once-famous band Shelter. Now Luna is in a band of her own, and Phoebe is trying to figure out her relationships with her whole family.

Patel, Sonia. *Rani Patel in Full Effect.* Cinco Puntos, 2016. After her Gujarati family's move to a remote Hawaiian island suspends them in cultural isolation, 16-year-old Rani Patel uses rap to forge an identity.

Prinz, Yvonne. *The Vinyl Princess.* HarperTeen, 2010. Allie, a self-professed music geek, works at a used record store in Berkeley, and her life is all about love, blogging, music and her not-always-easy relationship with her mother.

Rubens, Michael. *The Bad Decisions Playlist.* Clarion, 2016. Austin, 16, has just learned that the father he thought was dead is, in fact, Shane Tyler, a famous singer/guitarist/song writer. What's more, Shane has just showed up in Austin's hometown of Minneapolis to record an album.

Sales, Leila. *This Song Will Save Your Life.* Egmont, 2013. Nearly a year after a failed suicide attempt, 16-year-old Elise discovers that she has the passion, and the talent, to be a disc jockey.

Vlahos, Len. *The Scar Boys.* Egmont, 2014. Harry has scars both physical and emotional from a lightning strike when he was a child. Now he's a member of a band called The Scar Boys.

Walker, Melissa C. *Lovestruck Summer.* HarperTeen, 2009. Quinn is an indie rock girl who arrives in Austin, Texas, for a summer music internship—and she's determined to find her ideal boyfriend while she's there.

MAKE ME CRY

Use a background of teardrops, tissue boxes, and sad faces. Include an actual tissue box in the display.

Asher, Jay. *13 Reasons Why.* Razorbill, 2008. When Clay Jenkins receives a box containing 13 cassette tapes recorded by his classmate Hannah, who committed suicide, he spends a bewildering and heartbreaking night crisscrossing their town, listening to Hannah's voice recounting the events leading up to her death.

Forman, Gayle. *I Was Here.* Viking, 2015. In an attempt to understand why her best friend committed suicide, Cody retraces her dead friend's footsteps and makes some startling discoveries.

Forman, Gayle. *If I Stay.* Dutton, 2009. In a coma following an automobile accident that killed her parents and younger brother, 17-year-old Mia, a gifted cellist, weighs whether to live with her grief or join her family in death.

Green, John. *The Fault in Our Stars.* Dutton, 2012. Hazel and Gus meet in a support group for teens with cancer.

Hinton, S.E. *The Outsiders*. Viking, 1967. Three brothers struggle to stay together after the death of their parents.

Kantor, Melissa. *Maybe One Day*. HarperTeen, 2014. When Zoe's best friend Olivia is diagnosed with a life-threatening disease, Zoe quickly learns that priorities change.

Ness, Patrick. *A Monster Calls*. Candlewick, 2011. Thirteen-year-old Conor awakens one night to find a monster outside his bedroom window, but not the one from the recurring nightmare that began when his mother became ill—an ancient, wild creature that wants him to face truth and loss.

Oliver, Lauren. *Before I Fall*. Harper, 2010. After she dies in a car crash, teenage Samantha relives the day of her death over and over again until, on the seventh day, she finally discovers a way to save herself.

Schmidt, Gary D. *Orbiting Jupiter*. Clarion, 2015. Fourteen-year-old foster child Joseph wants nothing more than to find his daughter, Jupiter, whom he has never met.

Wein, Elizabeth. *Code Name Verity*. Hyperion, 2012. In 1943, a British fighter plane crashes in Nazi-occupied France and the survivor tells a tale of friendship, war, espionage, and great courage as she relates what she must to survive while keeping secret all that she can.

Yoon, Nicola. *Everything, Everything*. Delacorte, 2015. A teenage girl who's literally allergic to the outside world begins a complicated romance with her next-door neighbor who challenges everything she's ever known.

Yoon, Nicola. *The Sun Is Also a Star*. Delacorte, 2016. Natasha believes in science and facts. Daniel has always been a good son and good student. When they meet, it seems there is something extraordinary in store for both of them.

MERMAIDS, SIRENS, SEA CREATURES

Use an ocean background; include pictures of mermaids and other sea creatures. If possible, decorate with shells and sand.

Brown, Anne Greenwood. *Lies Beneath*. Delacorte, 2012. As the only brother in a family of mermaids, Calder is expected to seduce Lily, whose father killed the mermaids' mother, but he begins to fall in love with her just as Lily starts to suspect the legends about the lake are true.

Childs, Tera Lynn. *Forgive My Fins*. Katherine Tegan, 2012. Seventeen-year-old Lily, half-mermaid and half-human, has been living on land and attending high school, where she develops a crush on a boy but is afraid to tell him of her true destiny as the ruler of the undersea kingdom of Thalassinia.

Cordova, Zoraida. *The Vicious Deep*. Sourcebooks Fire, 2012. After being sucked out to sea in a tidal wave, Tristan returns ashore on Coney Island with no memory of what happened to him—yet, he can sense the emotions of others and dreams of a terrifying silver mermaid with razor-sharp teeth.

Cornwell, Betsy. *Tides*. Clarion, 2013. On the Isles of Shoals for a marine biology internship, 18-year-old Noah learns of his grandmother's romance with a selkie woman, falls for the selkie's daughter, and must work with her to rescue her siblings from his mentor's cruel experiments.

Davies, Anna. *Wrecked.* Simon & Schuster, 2012. When a boating accident off Whym Island, South Carolina, takes the lives of four friends and injures three others, 17-year-old Miranda meets Christian, a sort of merman who saved her life but was then charged by a sea witch to kill her.

Fama, Elizabeth. *Monstrous Beauty.* Farrar, Straus and Giroux, 2012. Syrenka is a mermaid—a fierce, seductive, beautiful, immortal creature of the sea who is willing to sacrifice anything for a chance at love in the 18th century. Hester is a 21st-century teenager whose story intertwines with Syrenka's in this tale of magic, myth, history, curses, and murder.

Howard, Amalie. *Waterfell.* Harlequin Teen, 2013. Disguised as a human while waiting for the day she can claim her birthright as heir to her murdered father's undersea kingdom, Nerissa is challenged to a battle to the death by her family's betrayer when she comes of age.

Lanagan, Margo. *The Brides of Rollrock Island.* Knopf, 2012. Rollrock Island is a strange place where seals loiter about, giving rise to the legend of beautiful brides emerging from these seals, only to pine for the ocean every waking hour they spend away from it.

Madison, Bennett. *September Girls.* HarperTeen, 2013. Vacationing in a sleepy beach town for the summer, Sam is pursued by hordes of blonde girls before falling in love with the unusual DeeDee, who compels him to uncover secrets about the community's ocean-dwelling inhabitants.

Moskowitz, Hannah. *Teeth.* Simon Pulse, 2013. Rudy's life is flipped upside-down when his family moves to a remote, magical island in a last attempt to save his sick younger brother, Dylan.

Napoli, Donna Jo. *Sirena.* Scholastic, 2000. When Sirena and her sisters sing their songs to the sailors on their way to the Trojan War, the men crash their ships upon the rocks.

Pearce, Jackson. *Fathomless.* Little, Brown, 2012. Celia, who shares mental powers with her triplet sisters, finds competition for a handsome boy with Lo, a sea monster who must persuade a mortal to love her and steal his soul to earn back her humanity.

Reese, Jenn. *Above World.* Candlewick, 2012. In a future of high technology and genetic modification the Coral Kampii, like legendary mermaids, live isolated from the Above World, but when the devices that allows them to breathe underwater start to fail, 13-year-old Aluna and her friend Hoku go to that forbidden place to find help.

Rosenfeld, Kat. *Inland.* Dutton, 2014. Returning to the coast after living in the Midwest, Callie's mysterious illness disappears, but when the water near her house begins to call her, she uncovers dangerous family secrets and jeopardizes everything and everyone she holds dear.

Souders, J. A. *Renegade.* Tor Teen, 2012. Trained since the age of three to be Daughter of the People, 16-year-old Evelyn Winters believes her underwater world of Elysium is perfect until Gavin Hunter, a surface Dweller, stumbles into Elysium and she realizes that everything she knows is a lie perpetrated by "Mother."

OTHER DISPLAY IDEAS

The more you work with teen collections, the more you will begin to notice trends and similarities in book covers. These similarities can make great displays. Just collect a bunch of books with some common theme on the cover and display them. If possible, come up with a clever title. Here are some examples of cover-related displays:

- "Red" a good book lately? (books with red covers)
- "Orange" you glad you came to the library today? (books with orange covers)
- Am I blue? (blue covers)
- I can't remember the title, but the cover was green (green covers)
- A rainbow of reading (variety of colors, preferably in rainbow order)
- From the heart (books with hearts on the cover)
- Dude, where's my head? (books on which the cover model's head is not shown or only partially shown, for example, *Cross My Heart and Hope to Spy*, by Ally Carter or *Along for the Ride*, by Sarah Dessen)
- Girls in gowns (e.g., *Shatter Me*, by Tahereh Mafi or *Bewitching*, by Alex Flinn)
- I'll be back (covers featuring the back of the cover model, e.g., *I Was Here*, by Gayle Forman or *Better Than Perfect*, by Melissa Kantor)
- It's sunny out there (sunglasses, e.g., *The Disenchantments*, by Nina Lacour or *Heist Society*, by Ally Carter)

FURTHER READING

ALA. 2015. *Intellectual Freedom Manual*, 9th edition. Chicago: ALA Editions.

Alessio, Amy, ed. 2008. *Excellence in Library Services to Young Adults*, 5th edition. Chicago: YALSA.

Alessio, Amy and Kimberly Patton. 2011. *A Year of Programs for Teens 2*. Chicago: ALA Editions.

Alexander, Linda B. and Nahyun Kwon, eds. 2010. *Multicultural Programming for Tweens and Teens*. Chicago: ALA Editions.

Bartel, Julie and Pamela Spencer Holley. 2010. *YALSA Annotated Book Lists for Every Teen Reader: The Best from the Experts at YALSA-BK*. New York: Neal-Schuman.

Blakemore, Sarah Jayne. June 2012. "The Mysterious Workings of the Adolescent Brain." Available at: www.ted.com/talks/sarah_jayne_blakemore_the_mysterious_workings_of_the_adolescent_brain.html.

Booth, Heather. 2007. *Serving Teens through Readers' Advisory*. Chicago: ALA Editions.

Braun, Linda. 2011. "The Importance of a Whole Library Approach to Public Library Young Adult Services." Available at: www.ala.org/yalsa/guidelines/whitepapers/wholelibrary.

Braun, Linda W. 2012. *Being a Teen Library Services Advocate*. Chicago: ALA/Neal-Schuman.

Braun, Linda, Hillias J. Martin, and Connie Urquhart. 2010. *Risky Business: Taking and Managing Risks in Library Service to Teens*. Chicago: ALA Editions.

Burek Pierce, Jennifer. 2007. *Sex, Brains, and Video Games: The Librarian's Guide to Teens in the Twenty-First Century*. Chicago: ALA Editions.

Business Insider. December 26, 2015. "How to Sell Yourself in 30 Seconds and Leave People Wanting More." Available at: http://www.businessinsider.com/how-to-give-a-30-second-elevator-pitch-2015-12.

Cart, Michael. 2010. *Young Adult Literature: From Romance to Realism*. Chicago: ALA Editions.

Coleman, Tina and Peggie Llanes. 2013. *The Hipster Librarian Guide to Teen Craft Projects 2*. Chicago: ALA Editions.

Dahl, Melissa. March 12, 2015. "Age 12 Is Like a Second Toddlerhood." *New York Magazine*. Available at: http://nymag.com/scienceofus/2015/03/age-12-is-like-a-second-toddlerhood.html#.

Dobbs, David. October 2011. "Beautiful Brains." *National Geographic*. Available at: http://ngm.nationalgeographic.com/print/2011/10/teenage-brains/dobbs-text.

Eagle, mk. 2012. *Answering Teens' Tough Questions*. Chicago: ALA/Neal-Schuman.

Fink, Megan, ed. 2011. *Teen Read Week and Teen Tech Week: Tips and Resources for YALSA's Initiatives*. Chicago: YALSA.

Flowers, Sarah. 2012. *Evaluating Teen Services and Programs*. Chicago: ALA/Neal-Schuman.

Gorman, Michele and Tricia Suellentrop. 2009. *Connecting Young Adults and Libraries: A How-to-Do-It Manual*, 4th edition. New York: Neal-Schuman.

Harper, Meghan. 2010. *Reference Sources and Services for Youth*. New York: Neal-Schuman.

Harris, Frances Jacobson. 2010. *I Found It on the Internet: Coming of Age Online*, 2nd edition. Chicago: ALA Editions.

Helmrich, Erin and Elizabeth Schneider. 2011. *Create, Relate, and Pop @ the Library: Services and Programs for Teens & Tweens*. New York: Neal-Schuman.

Herald, Diana Tixier. 2010. *Teen Genreflecting 3: A Guide to Reading Interests*. Santa Barbara, CA: Libraries Unlimited.

Holley, Pamela Spencer. 2010. *Quick and Popular Reads for Teens*. Chicago: ALA Editions.

Lillian, Jenine, ed. 2009. *Cool Teen Programs for Under $100*. Chicago: YALSA.

Mahood, Kristine. 2010. *Booktalking with Teens*. Santa Barbara, CA: Libraries Unlimited.

Office of Intellectual Freedom. 2010. *Privacy and Freedom of Information in 21st Century Libraries*. Chicago: ALA TechSource.

Ott, Valerie. 2006. *Teen Programs with Punch: A Month-by-Month Guide*. Westport, CT: Libraries Unlimited.

Palfrey, John and Urs Gasser. 2008. *Born Digital: Understanding the First Generation of Digital Natives*. New York: Basic Books.

Ross, Catherine Sheldrick, Kirsti Nilsen, and Marie L. Radford. 2009. *Conducting the Reference Interview: A How-to-Do-It Manual for Librarians*, 2nd edition. New York: Neal-Schuman.

Schwartz, Katrina. December 21, 2015. "Harnessing the Incredible Learning Potential of the Adolescent Brain." Available at: http://ww2.kqed.org/mindshift/2015/12/21/harnessing-the-incredible-learning-potential-of-the-adolescent-brain/.

Starkey, Monique Delatte, ed. 2013. *Practical Programming: The Best of YA-YAAC*. Chicago: YALSA.

Strauch, Barbara. 2003. *The Primal Teen*. New York: Doubleday.

Sullivan, Michael. 2010. *Serving Boys through Readers' Advisory*. Chicago: ALA Editions.

Tuccillo, Diane P. 2010. *Teen-Centered Library Service: Putting Youth Participation into Practice*. Santa Barbara, CA: Libraries Unlimited.

Welch, Rollie James. 2010. *A Core Collection for Young Adults*, 2nd edition. New York: Neal-Schuman.

WNYC. 2015. "Being 12: The Year Everything Changes." Available at: www.wnyc.org/series/being-12/.

YALSA. 2008. "Guidelines for Library Services to Teens." Available at: http://www.ala.org/yalsa/sites/ala.org.yalsa/files/content/ReferenceGuidelines_0308.pdf.

YALSA. 2011a. "Competencies for Librarians Serving Youth." Available at: www.ala.org/yalsa/sites/ala.org.yalsa/files/content/guidelines/yadeservethebest_201.pdf.

YALSA. 2011b. "Public Library Evaluation Tool." Available at: www.ala.org/yalsa/sites/ala.org.yalsa/files/content/guidelines/yacompetencies/evaluationtool.pdf.

YALSA. 2012a. *The Complete Summer Reading Manual: From Planning to Evaluation*. Chicago: YALSA.

YALSA. 2015. "Core Professional Values for the Teen Services Profession." Available at: www.ala.org/yalsa/core-professional-values-teen-services-profession.

INDEX

Abstract thought, 2–3, 12, 33, 36
Adobe Photoshop, 43
Adult Books 4 Teens, 28, 91
Advise and Consent, 45
Advocacy for teens, 70–72
Advocacy Toolkit, 71
ALA (American Library Association), 4, 45, 68, 88
Alex Award, 29
All the King's Men, 45
All the President's Men, 45
Almost Astronauts, 30
ALSC (Association of Library Service to Children), 6, 25, 72
Amazing Audiobooks, 29, 90
Amazon, 26, 81
American Library Association (ALA), 4, 45, 68, 88
American Psychological Association, 12
Amygdala, 2, 13
Anger, 13, 17
Anime, 22, 26
Annie E. Casey Foundation, 6
Appeal factors in readers' advisory, 27–28
Arduino, 43
Aronson, Marc, 21, 25
Art shows, 36
Association for Library Service to Children (ALSC), 6, 25, 72
Audiobooks, 23, 25, 29, 36, 63
Audrey, Wait, 30
Author visits, 37

Baker & Taylor, 28
Battle of the bands, 36
BBC Radio, 4, 54
Behavior, 8, 11–18, 76; distracting vs. dangerous, 16–18; ethical, 70; inappropriate, 76; information-seeking, 49–50, 51; online, 69–70
Benway, Robin, 30
Berkman Center for Internet and Society, 57, 69

Bernier, Anthony, 62
Best Fiction for Young Adults, 23, 29, 94
Blogs, 28–29, 89–90, 91; Heavy Medal, 91; Hub, The, 28, 89; No Flying, No Tights, 28; Reading While White, 92; Someday My Printz Will Come, 28, 91; Stacked, 28; Teen Librarian Toolbox, 91; We Need Diverse Books, 92; YALSABlog, 89
Bolan, Kimberly, 59
Bomb: The Race to Build—and Steal—the World's Most Dangerous Weapon, 30
BookBrowse, 29
Book clubs, 36, 103–4
Book displays, 32, 63, 77
Book faces, 42
Booklist, 26, 29, 91, 92
Booklist Online, 29
Booklists, 23, 28, 29, 32, 90, 91
Booktalking, 29–32
Book trailers, 28, 32, 77
Brain, 1–3, 4, 5, 12, 13, 14, 36; anatomy, 2–3; and behavior, 11–12, 14
Brainfuse, 57
Brainstem, 2
Brainstorm: The Power and Purpose of the Teenage Brain, 2, 3, 8, 13, 14, 17
Bray, Libba, 30
Budget: professional development, 93; programs about, 37, 40; teen services and programs, 22, 39, 40, 53, 64
Bunce, Elizabeth, 30
Burkey, Mary, 25

Caldecott Award, 24, 93
Candidate, The, 45
Candidates, political, 45
Career Builder, 43
Cerebellum, 2
Cerebral cortex, 2, 12
Cerebrum, 2
Charlotte Mecklenburg Library, 62, 71
Chast, Roz, 24

Circadian rhythms, 2
Collection development policies, 22, 53, 63, 66
College readiness, 44
Comic books, 24
Committees, professional, 94, 95
Community engagement, 37
Computer filters, 68
Conflict resolution, 8, 13
Connected learning, 4, 18, 36, 43, 59
Connected Learning Research Network, 4
Cooperative Children's Book Center, 25
Copyright, 70
Cortex, 2, 12, 14
Crafts, 36, 37, 76, 77, 81
"Crash Course" YouTube Channel, 54
Creative Commons, 70
Critical thinking, 12
Curriculum support, 22, 51
Curse Dark as Gold, A, 30

Dangerous behaviors, 16–17
Databases, 51, 52, 54, 55, 56
Databases, readers' advisory, 29
De la Peña, Matt, 26
Demco, 92
Developmental assets, 7–8, 18, 36, 38
Developmental stages, 1, 8, 17, 69, 82
Distracting behaviors, 16–17
Diversity, collection, 25–26, 82, 92
Diversity, in the teen population, 6–7, 82, 92
Donations, for library events, 40

eBooks, 6
EBSCO, 29
Edelweiss, 26
Elected officials, 71, 72
Election, 45
Elevator speeches, 71–72
Emotions of teens, 2, 3, 4, 8, 13, 19
Empowerment, 8, 14, 38
Entertainment Weekly, 23
E! Online, 23
Epic Reads (website), 28
Ethics, information, 55
Ethics, library, 81
Evaluation of programs, 38, 39, 41
Excellence in Nonfiction for Young Adults
     Award, 23, 29

Facebook, 5, 40, 57, 77, 78, 81, 92
Facial expressions, 13–14, 23, 49
Fama, Elizabeth, 30
Filmmaking, 43
Financial aid, 44
Follett, 28
Forebrain, 2
Freedom of speech, 65
Friends of the Library, 39, 72
Frontal lobe, 2
Furness, Adrienne, 56
Furniture for teen spaces, 16, 61, 63
Future of Library Services for and with Teens,
     7, 88

Galleys, 26
Games: board, 7, 37, 38; college readiness, 44;
     computer, 6, 23, 37, 70; console, 7, 22, 37
GarageBand, 43
Gasser, Urs, 69
Gender, 17, 25, 27
Genres, 7, 21, 22, 24, 26, 27, 29, 33, 36
GN4LIB, 26
Going Bovine, 30
Goldsmith, Francisca, 23
Goodreads, 26, 31
Google, 5, 50, 56, 57
Grants, 40, 90
Graphic novels, 22, 23–25, 26, 28, 29, 91, 99
Great Graphic Novels for Young Adults, 29, 94
Green, Hank, 54
Green, John, 32, 54

HALT (Hungry, Angry, Lonely, Tired), 17–18
Harry Potter series, 4, 42
Harvard University, 57
Heavy Medal blog, 91
Helping Homeschoolers in the Library, 56
Hindbrain, 2
Hippocampus, 2
History Channel, The, 54
Hogwarts at Ravelry, 4
Homeschooling, 55–56
Homework, 17, 26, 50–54
Homework alerts, 52
Homework Help from the Library, 52
Hormones, 3, 4
Hub, The (blog), 28, 89–90, 91

Hunger, 2, 17
Hunger Games series, The, 28, 104
Hypothalamus, 2

Identity, online, 69
Identity, sense of, 8, 12, 15
Imposed queries, 50, 56
Infopeople, 92, 95
Information literacy, 51, 55, 70
Information-seeking behavior, 49–50, 51
Ingram, 28
In Our Time podcast, 54
Intellectual freedom, 65, 82
Intner, Carol, 52
iTunes, 54, 81

Jensen, Frances, 3
Jobs for teens, 43, 44; at the library,
    81–82; for volunteers, 77–78
*Journal of Research on Libraries and
    Young Adults,* 4, 89

Khan Academy, 54
King County (WA) Library, 53
Kuhlmann, Meghann, 60

Labor Unions, 77, 95
Leadership, 71, 95
League of Women Voters, 45
Lee and Low Books, 25
Library Bill of Rights, 65, 66
Library Journal, 26, 91, 92
Library of Congress, 54
Library Thing, 26, 31
Life skills, 37, 44
Limbic system, 2, 3, 13
Lincoln, 45
LMMS software, 43
Lock-ins, 38
Loft, The, 62
Loneliness, 17
Los Angeles Public Library, 53

Magazines, 23, 26, 63, 77
Makerspaces, 42, 43
Males, Mike, 62
The Manchurian Candidate, 45
Manga, 22, 24, 25, 26

Martin, Crystle, 4
Melatonin, 4–5
Michael L. Printz Award, 23, 28, 29,
    91, 93
Midbrain, 2
Millennials, 5
Monstrous Beauty, 30
Monstrumologist, The, 30
Morris Award, 23, 29, 32
Mr. Smith Goes to Washington, 45
Multicultural books, 25–26, 92

Naidoo, Jamie Campbell, 25
National Center for Education
    Statistics, 55
National Forum on Teens and Libraries,
    3, 5
National Geographic, 54
National Sleep Foundation, 4
National Teen Space Guidelines, 60
NetGalley, 26
Newbery Award, 24, 26, 91–92, 93
Nielsen Company, 6
No Flying, No Tights blog, 28
Nonfiction, in YA collections, 21, 22, 24,
    25, 26, 27, 63
Nonfiction Award. *See* Excellence in
    Nonfiction for Young Adults Award
Nonfiction booktalks, 30
Nonfiction Honor List, VOYA, 91
Nonfiction readers' advisory, 25, 26,
    27, 30
NoveList, 29

Occipital lobe, 2
Ochsner, Amanda, 44
OCLC, 57
Odyssey Award, 29
Online safety, 69
Osborne, Charli, 63–64

Palfrey, John, 69
Parietal lobe, 2
Passive programs, 36, 41–42, 45
Pathfinders, 53
PBS, 54
Peer groups, 8, 12, 14, 15, 16, 17, 68, 69
People, 23

Personal queries, 50, 54–55
Pew Research Center, 5, 57
Photography, 36, 37
Pinterest, 32, 42, 43
Plagiarism, 70
Planning (as a brain function), 2, 8
Planning programs for teens, 37, 38–39, 41, 45
Planning teen spaces, 60,
Planning volunteer programs, 78
Podcasts, 23, 54, 71
Poetry, 42
Policies, library, 59, 61, 63, 65, 66, 67, 68, 69
Popular: Vintage Wisdom for a Modern Geek, 30
Popular Paperbacks for Young Adults, 29
Prefrontal cortex, 2, 14
Printz Award. *See* Michael L. Printz Award
Problem novels, 21
Professional development plan, 95
Professional growth and development, 87–93
Professional organizations, 87–90
Program costs, 39–40
Programs for teens, 35–47
Project Vote Smart, 45
Promotion of library events, 38, 39
Pruning, neural, 3
Public Broadcasting System, 54
Publicity and marketing, 38, 39, 40
Public Library Association, 93, 101
Public Library Evaluation Tool, 88
Publishers Weekly, 26, 91
Pullias Center for Higher Education, 44

Quick Picks for Reluctant Young Adult Readers, 23, 29, 90

Rainie, Lee, 5, 6
Raspberry Pi, 43
Read-alikes, 28
Readers' advisory, 12, 23, 24, 26–29, 32, 33, 82, 89, 91
Readers' theater, 38, 78
Reading While White blog, 92
Reasoning, abstract, 2–3, 12, 33, 36
Reasoning, critical, 2, 12, 14, 61
Recreational activities for teens, 35, 43
Recreational reading, 21, 22, 26, 27, 50
RedBox, 81
Reference, virtual, 57

Reference interview, 12, 13, 23, 53–54, 58
Reference questions, 23, 49, 54, 55
Reluctant readers, 23, 24, 29
Resumés, 44
Revolver, 29
Right to privacy, 65, 67, 68, 69
Robotics, 12, 43
Rookie Magazine, 23

San Francisco Public Library, 53
Scavenger hunts, 42
School librarians, 51, 55, 91
School Library Journal, 26, 28, 91, 92
Scratch software, 43
Search Institute, 7–8
Seating in teen spaces, 62–63
Sedgwick, Marcus, 29
Selection resources, 26, 91
Seven Days in May, 45
Sexuality, 2, 50, 54
Sheinkin, Steve, 30
Siegel, Daniel, 2, 3, 8, 13, 14, 17
Sightlines, 62
Sketchup software, 43
Sleep deprivation, 4–5, 18
Smartphones, 6, 25, 36, 37, 41, 57
Smart Voting Starts @ Your Library, 45
Social networking, 50, 57, 70
Someday My Printz Will Come blog, 28, 91
Space Guidelines. *See* National Teen Space Guidelines
Stacked (website), 28, 92
StarCraft, 4
STEM (Science, Technology, Engineering, Math), 43, 89
Stone, Tanya Lee, 30
Superheroes, 24
Surveys, evaluation, 38, 41
Synapses, 3

Teen advisory boards, 18–19, 22, 37, 38, 40, 71, 82, 89
Teen participation, 18–19, 60
Teen Read Week, 72
Teen Services Underground, 29
Teen spaces, 59–64
Teens' Top Ten, 32
Teen Tech Week, 72

Teen Vogue, 23
Teen volunteers. *See* Volunteers, teen
Temporal lobe, 2
Test preparation, 37, 43
Texas State Library and Archives
        Commission, 92, 95
Textbooks, 22, 53
Thalamus, 2
Tiredness, 18
TMZ, 23
Top Shelf Fiction for Middle School
        Readers, VOYA, 91
Transliteracy, 23
Tumblr, 92
Tutor.com, 57
Twilight, 28
Twitter, 40, 42, 57, 92

Unions, 77, 95
University of California (Berkeley), 56
University of Southern California, 44

Van Wagenen, Maya, 30
Voice of Youth Advocates (VOYA), 26, 91
Volunteer jobs, 77–81
Volunteers, teen, 75–81
VOYA. See Voice of Youth Advocates

Wag the Dog, 45
Walker, Sally M., 30

Webinars, 89, 92, 95
Webjunction, 92
Website evaluation, 55–56
Websites for readers' advisory, 28–29,
        89–91
Websites for teen programming,
        46–48
We Need Diverse Books (website),
        25, 92
Wikipedia, 5, 50, 56, 57
Workforce development, 43–44
WorldCat, 57
Writing contests, 36
Written in Bone, 30

YALSA (Young Adult Library Services
        Association), 4, 5, 6, 7, 23, 26, 28,
        29, 32, 40, 42, 43, 59, 60, 71, 72,
        88–90, 91, 92, 93, 94, 95
YALSA-BK, 26, 89
YALSABlog, 91
Yancey, Rick, 30
Young Adult Library Services (YALS),
        44, 89
Young Adult Library Services
        Association. *See* YALSA
Young adult literature, definition,
        21–22
Young Adult Services Symposium, 93
YouTube, 5, 22, 54, 71, 77, 89

ABOUT THE AUTHOR

SARAH FLOWERS is the retired deputy county librarian at the Santa Clara County Library. She currently teaches online courses on teen services and supervision for Infopeople. She was a member of the top 40 distinguished alumni of the San Jose State School of Library and Information Science and one of the first *Library Journal* "Movers and Shakers." Flowers is the author of numerous articles and reviews for library journals, as well as the author of *Young Adults Deserve the Best: YALSA's Competencies in Action* and *Evaluating Teen Services and Programs*. She has been active in ALA and YALSA (Young Adult Library Services Association) for many years and was president of YALSA 2011–2012.